12 Squadron at RAF B
L
Good ex-lc

EIGHT
FIFTY

27

THE TURRETS OF WAR

THE TURRETS OF WAR

Douglas Eades

JANUS PUBLISHING COMPANY
London, England

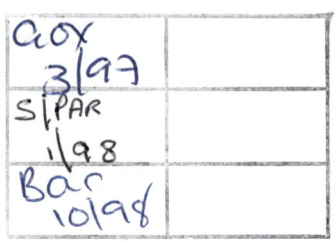

First published in Great Britain 1996
by Janus Publishing Company,
Edinburgh House, 19 Nassau Street,
London W1N 7RE

Copyright © Douglas Eades 1996

**British Library Cataloguing-in-Publication Data.
A catalogue record for this book is available from the
British Library.**

ISBN 1 85756 266 6

All rights reserved. No part of this publication may be
reproduced, stored in a retrieval system or transmitted in
any form or by any means, electronic, mechanical,
photocopying, recording or otherwise, without the prior
permission of the publisher.

The right of Douglas Eades to be identified
as the author of this work has been asserted by him
in accordance with the Copyright, Designs and Patents
Act 1988.

Printed and bound in England by
Antony Rowe Ltd,
Chippenham, Wiltshire

To CHIC
With love and gratitude for facing with fortitude the possibility of receiving a fateful official telegram and remaining cheerful throughout the long and lonesome periods of the war.

Contents

	Acknowledgements	ix
	Foreword	xi
	Glossary	xiii
	Introduction	1
1	Early Days	5
2	The Balloon Goes Up	9
3	Taking a Chance Lightly	21
4	Initial Training	29
5	Coloured Holes Count	33
6	Circuits and Bumps	39
7	The Curtain Rises	47
8	The Big One	55
9	Fear Is an Ally	59
10	Germany 4 Italy 2	65
11	A Low Blow	73
12	Some Surprises	85
13	The (Un)happy Valley	99
14	A Rest Period	123
15	A Second Tour	143
	Afterthoughts	167
	Appendices	177
	Bibliography	181

Acknowledgements

It is a pleasure to mention a few of many friends and colleagues who provided information and photographs and helped generally in the preparation of my work. Amongst ex-12 Squadron members my thanks go to Ken Swann, Jo Lancaster, Laurie Lawrence, Edward Martin (Photographic Records) and Jim MacDonald; to my first tour skipper Maurice Wells, and Harry Moreton (FE) his right-hand man. From elsewhere my thanks to Harry Flack, John Chambers (THE Defiant fighter expert) Desi Shaw and Jim Patterson. My special thanks to my lifelong friend George (not forgetting his noble intermediate initials – HM) Richardson; to Jim Hampton for introducing me to Ted Hooton without whose help the book, in all probability, would never have been published! I have also to thank many others who have read these pages and commented on them, including Jim Heyworth who, in addition, provided the Foreword.

Foreword

It is unusual to read about flying operations in Bomber Command from the point of view of an air gunner and it has been an opportunity for me to turn back the pages of life to my second tour of operations with 12 Squadron during the spring and summer of 1943. This was a period when there was a great increase in striking capacity of the bomber force, under the command of Air Chief Marshal Sir Arthur Harris, whose efforts helped to turn the tide of the Second World War.

The official statistics of aircrew losses on Bomber Command squadrons were high and confidence was the key to maintaining good morale in a crew to restrict those losses. Confidence stemmed from two sources – the thorough maintenance of aircraft by servicing crews to provide a reliable bomber and a competent aircrew with clear airborne discipline.

Maurice Wells and his crew, in which Doug Eades served as a mid-upper gunner, caught the full blast of the offensive against the Ruhr, which they visited 17 times in a relatively short period of a few weeks. Doug's description of these raids and especially of life in general for aircrew is written in a form not previously attempted and I commend it as a fair representation of squadron life during those exciting and fearsome days.

Jim Heyworth
formerly Squadron Leader
Officer Commanding B Flight
12 Squadron

Glossary

GENERAL

bod or erk:	an airman
cookie:	4,000lb bomb
flak:	enemy anti-aircraft fire (contraction of *Fliegerabwehrkanonen*)
Happy Valley:	the Ruhr
intercom:	communication link between the crew in the aircraft
NAAFI:	canteen
op(s):	bombing operation(s)
PFF:	Pathfinder Force
station:	RAF base
TI:	target indicator ground marker

CLOUDS

10/10ths:	complete cloud coverage – 5/10ths half cover and so on

RANKS

Winco:	Wing Commander
F/Lt:	Flight Lieutenant
F/O:	Flying Officer

DIRECTIONS

starboard:	right side of aircraft looking forward
port:	left side of aircraft looking forward
beam:	at right angles to or across the fuselage
bow:	45 degrees forward of the beam
quarter:	45 degrees aft of the beam

LUFTWAFFE FIGHTERS

Fw 190:	Focke-Wulf 190
Ju 88:	Junkers 88
Me 109:	Messerschmitt 109
Me 110:	Messerschmitt 110

RAF BOMBERS

Halifax:	Four-engined bomber, not quite as extensively used as the Lancaster
Lancaster:	Four-engined heavy bomber
Stirling:	Four-engined bomber, but taken off operational flying in 1944
Wellington:	Twin-engined medium bomber

The author ... Flying Officer Douglas Eades

Introduction

At the end of hostilities in 1945 the majority of the serving forces were pleased to be demobilised. The Royal Air Force had its attractions, of course, comradeship and adventure are only two examples from a long list of items I could compile and indeed many of my wartime colleagues signed on for various periods of regular service. This was not for me however and, late in 1945, after arriving home from India, my aim was to set about building a career and enjoy a settled married life which I had been denied for so many years. I quickly found myself a job and in the work-a-day world the war soon became irrelevant and almost forgotten. In view of this a reader might well wonder why I should decide to write a book on my wartime experiences nearly fifty years on. To what then do I attribute this paradox?

Well, it all started early in the 1980s when I heard in a roundabout way that an organisation named The Wickenby Register proposed to erect a memorial to the 1,080 young men of 12 and 626 Squadrons who had flown from their base at RAF Wickenby against German targets for the last time and had given their lives in an attempt to stop the onward march of the Nazi jackboot. As a wartime member of 12 Squadron I joined this organisation and eventually attended a very moving dedication ceremony. This experience and the opportunity to meet some wartime companions awakened my interest.

As a result, I began to realise that as a mid-upper gunner on Lancaster bombers I had taken part in a campaign that would prob-

The Icarus Memorial at RAF Wickenby

ably prove to be historically unique. The bombing of towns and cities in the First World War was relatively mild and quite unlike the Second World War in which sustained bombing was carried out by the Royal Air Force, the American Air Force and the Luftwaffe. Air raids by anything up to 1,000 heavy bombers per night became an outstanding feature but it seems unlikely that action on this scale will ever be witnessed again. The tendency these days is to use missiles of one type or another or faster smaller bombers carrying controlled bombs which were used with spectacular success in the Gulf War.

Those, like myself, who flew with Bomber Command forces are fast becoming a dying breed and, in the next few years many true stories will remain untold and, unfortunately, will be lost forever. I felt that I should not let this happen in my case and for this reason started to record for posterity my experiences in taking part in raids over Germany and elsewhere; to comment on how we lived; how we coped with fear and how we felt about the moral issues involved with area bombing. Much has been recorded of the facts. These can be read by anyone at the Public Record Office at Kew and, for example, in *The Bomber Command War Diaries* by Middlebrook and Everitt. Many books have been written about special incidents such as *The Dam Busters* or the *Peenemunde Raid*, but not so much seems to have been produced by individuals taking part in an ordinary tour of operations and more particularly by mid-upper air gunners, who were in an excellent position to observe events. As it happened I was involved, inter alia, in many raids on various locations in the Ruhr during the period March to June 1943. It became known as the Battle of the Ruhr although it was not seen as such at that time. It was a fascinating period of the war in which Bomber Command was often in the ascendency albeit at a cost of many lives.

However, before reading and judging for yourself, let me say that I have not jumped into describing the subject matter straight away. Instead I have gradually built up the story from the early days of the war and later through the training periods, side by side with my family life which I hope will assist a reader to appreciate the atmosphere and problems of those days more easily. Similarly, after describing operations, I continue the account until the end of the war, since

THE TURRETS OF WAR

I feel that it portrays, generally, the varied life of a member of aircrew in wartime.

Chapter 1

Early Days

In fine sunny weather, our little group of holiday makers, including my fiancée usually known as Chic, had enjoyed a week of rambling in the Lake District. Not a spot of rain had fallen and we had been free to roam the lanes or scramble amongst the hills day after day, confident that the weather was set fair and that the blue skies would continue to provide the right conditions for an open-air life. At the start of our second week, the Sunday morning dawned peacefully, with pockets of mist lying sleepily in the valleys between the hills overlooking Lake Windermere. The air was still, the sky clear and every promise of another fine day in Ambleside was in prospect. Unfortunately, the weather would have little effect on the events of the day.

The date was 3 September 1939 and the time was 11 a.m. Our companions, so full of happy chatter in the past week, had grown silent as we gathered around the radio to listen to Prime Minister Chamberlain make his historic announcement in which he said that, since the German Chancellor had ignored the ultimatum which had been issued earlier, our country was now at war with Germany. The silence amongst us continued as the strains of the national anthem died away. It was the end of all the uncertainty which had existed for the previous four years or so, during which time Hitler had ranted, raved and threatened all those who opposed his actions and policies. His massive rearmament programme and his aggressive entry into Poland had been too much... The limit had been reached.

That war had come was, for many of us, a relief. But, on looking back this seems a trifle odd since, in fact, the uncertainty about an impending war had only been replaced by a greater uncertainty about what the future might hold. Germany had been preparing for years and was militarily very strong. Britain was relatively weak and therefore vulnerable. Dangerous times were obviously ahead for both civilians and service personnel. Nevertheless, except for a few misguided pacifists, the vast majority of the nation held the view that right was on our side and come what might, the war had to be fought. It was now up to the younger members of the community to follow the footsteps of their fathers in the First World War and show what they could do.

Although we still had a week of our holiday to go, we decided that, in the circumstances, home was the better place to be. We would start for Sunderland that afternoon. Meanwhile Chic and I took a last lingering look at the countryside by walking slowly up to a favourite spot of ours on the Kirkstone Pass where we could enjoy a glimpse of Lake Windermere and Langdale Valley with its familiar and distinctive Pikes. Our panoramic and peaceful view was shattered suddenly by the wail of air-raid warning sirens in Ambleside. A small civil aircraft flew over the pass shortly afterwards and we looked at each other questioningly... A precursor of things to come perhaps? It certainly was for both of us but perhaps more so on my account since the sound of sirens and the sight of aircraft would become very much a part of my life in the years ahead.

It was with much regret later in the afternoon that, along with our friends George and Doreen, we pointed our Morris 12 in the homeward direction by making for Kendal. Here we stopped for some refreshment and were astonished to hear that Tyneside, some seven miles to the north of Sunderland as the crow flies, had been bombed... All codswallop, of course, but a pointer as to how rumours can fly in wartime. We arrived home during the evening to find everyone fully convinced that a raid was imminent. Logically, one could not dispute the fact that the north-east coastal towns of England were exposed and easy targets for any marauding enemy bombers. The night sky was clear and brilliantly moonlit – a positive bombers' moon – and Hitler would undoubtedly take swift revenge ... or so it was thought. Our fears were, of course, groundless and although great events took place in France and the Low Countries in the following months, Wearside did not experience enemy action until June 1940.

George and I, who had been friends since childhood, had only just missed being called-up in the militia some weeks earlier and now, at age 21, we would obviously be in the first group to be conscripted. We decided that the light blue uniform of the Royal Air Force was much better than khaki and, as neither of us had salt in our veins, the Navy held no attraction. We would therefore volunteer for the junior service at the first opportunity.

The next day we made our way to the local recruiting office and presented ourselves to the recruitment sergeant who was very receptive. The wheels began to turn astonishingly quickly. Almost immediately we were sent for medical examination and, having been pronounced fit, found that the skids had been smartly placed under us. We were told to report that evening and, on doing so, were promptly put on a train bound for Bedford. We travelled all night and arrived at RAF Cardington early the next morning. So in less than 48 hours of being on holiday we were sworn in as brand new aircraftsmen – AC plonks. It was now 5 September and I was allocated my new service number 935253 and told that I would be trained as a balloon rigger/fabric worker. Ye gods I thought, whoever concluded that this would be the best way I could serve the war effort? I suspect that Cardington, with its huge airship hangars where craft such as the R100 and R101 were built and which later had become the chief balloon centre, was somewhat biased towards its own genealogy. However that might be, George, always a good talker, had somehow wormed his way into being trained as a pilot but, since he had suffered a bout of enteritis some weeks previously, he could not pass the searching medical test and was sent home for two months in order to regain hundred per cent fitness. So we bade each other farewell at Cardington, little knowing that we would not meet again for three and a half years and in circumstances that neither of us could ever have been able to forecast.

As a squad of about one hundred, we were kitted out at Cardington. We were paraded, bullied and pushed around by a corporal known as Joe the Bastard, taught to use naughty, rude or crude words, pumped full of this and that inoculation serum, vaccinated and finally, with very sore arms were dispatched to RAF South Cerney, near Cirencester. As a permanent station it possessed good accommodation for regular staff but had little to offer this newly arrived stiff and very tired shower of rookies. Eventually, a large disused and dilapidated dining hall was made available to us. We were each issued with a palliasse, a minimum amount of straw, something very hard which served as a pillow and two blankets made from a coarse prickly material. Beds were not obtainable. The floor was good enough but the main difficulty was the draught which seemed to circulate and search out all corners of the hall regardless of our efforts to plug the air gaps. This was unfortunate, since the early autumn nights became progressively colder – much to our discomfort. However, the weather that September was exceptionally fine and warm by day, thus making life reasonably enjoyable. The training staff had no chance of making guardsmen out of us in four weeks of concentrated drilling and weapon training but I think this motley array of ex-civilians, drawn from all walks of life, were smartened up pretty well in the short space of time available and the passing-out parade appeared to be quite respectable. We had all learned to rough it and make the best of what we had. Certainly it does not take long, in the services, to discover that if you don't look after yourself, no one else will.

Chapter 2

The Balloon Goes Up

En route back to Cardington for balloon training, we had to change trains at Oxford and wait some hours for a train for Bedford. Cold weather had set in and we had no wish to stay in a cold and draughty railway station. However, someone remembered that Cooper's marmalade factory was not far away and a few of us decided that it might be a good idea to while away the time by asking if we could see their process plant. We sallied forth in a group and two of us were chosen to make our petition. A Yorkshire wag from 'uddersfield and myself approached the inquiry desk and tentatively made our request. After the rough life of the previous weeks it was gratifying to be received with courtesy. 'Please take a seat and I shall inquire', said the smiling receptionist. It looked promising and shortly we heard that the management were happy to show us around their plant and quickly organised a tour. We were then conducted around the factory and saw how they produced their various products which was interesting, but we also appreciated the warmth of our surroundings and pleasant cooking smells. Later, we were entertained in the boardroom by the managing director who finally presented each of us with two jars. One contained horseradish sauce and the other... chunky marmalade!

We arrived back at Cardington after midnight. In cold wind-driven rainy conditions it was early morning before the usual reception processes had been completed and sleeping accommodation found.

The hut allocated to us was reasonably warm and this was good but, better still, it contained beds. This indeed was luxury especially since we knew that many hundreds of airmen were sleeping in tents on the barrack square. Twelve hours had passed since we last consumed food and, unfortunately, the duty cook could not be found. The NAAFI canteen was closed, of course, and obviously we were not going to obtain food before the cookhouse opened at 6 a.m. Hunger pangs directed that we must have something to eat and the only alternative was to devour the horseradish sauce and marmalade, which we did at about 2.30 a.m. Perhaps to some it would appear similar to mixing treacle with kippers but, eaten with the aid of a knife, the two commodities seemed to complement each other and tasted quite well. At that time I reflected that, when really hungry, all food tastes good but I now further reflect that our digestive systems must have been in good shape to deal with this very acidic mixture in the middle of the night without any ill effects, and certainly it did not prevent us from sleeping soundly in our new comfortable beds.

Our training on balloon maintenance began the next day. The introduction of the course quickly dispelled the idea that these dumpy objects were useless and only served as a navigational aid to enemy bomber crews. At the start of the war, balloon barrages appeared over most of our larger towns and cities especially those in industrial areas. Their main function was to prevent or deter low-level bombing attacks on industry producing vital equipment needed for the war effort – ships, planes, transport and machinery, for example. Equally important, they obliged German bombers to fly at a height at which our anti-aircraft guns and searchlights could effectively deal with them. Balloons were attached to mobile winches by wire cables and could fly to a height of 6,000 feet but the normal operational height was 4,500 feet. It was not generally known that each end of the cable had attachments which would sever the wire if hit. Thus, any aircraft flying into the cable would either be brought down immediately or, if not, would carry away a length of heavy cable which, depending on its position, could make flying difficult. Ships, of course, often carried balloons for protection and, in the latter stages in the war, balloons achieved some success in forming a defensive line against doodlebugs. At one time a small number of what were called 'giraffe'

THE BALLOON GOES UP

A barrage balloon

A convoy lorry with two gas-bottle trailers

balloons were introduced. These could fly – I think – at 16,000 feet but they were not used much for technical reasons.

Balloons were tough enough to stand up to normal weather conditions but it was envisaged that for wartime operational requirements they would, in an emergency, have to be flown in adverse weather. As the damage factor was expected to be high and if full operational strengths were to be maintained there was an obvious need to train a large number of repair crews. This is where we came in – we would be trained as balloon riggers and fabric workers and, as such, would help to keep the balloon squadrons up to strength. The course was much more interesting than would appear on the surface. The terminology and style had a distinctly naval flavour about it, possibly stemming from the sailing-ship era. On the practical side, I found that sewing and patching fabric, and splicing wire and ropes was a quite skilful occupation. Additionally, the RAF's attention to the depth of knowledge and detail on the theory of use and handling of balloons was quite absorbing. Practical training was carried out in the two vast airship hangars. If I remember correctly they were 200 feet high and each covered about seven acres. At the bottom end of the first hangar a cross section of one of the old airships had been hung and preserved, presumably, for posterity. Although historically interesting, the hangars had no heating and in November seemed to attract arctic conditions. They really were cold – enough to be dangerous to brass monkeys – and I, in common with others, was always pleased to return to the lecture rooms.

At the end of our training, with indecent haste, we were split into groups and dispatched to various centres around the country. I was assigned to No 5 Balloon Centre at Sutton Coldfield. This unit was responsible for the control of 911, 912 and 913 (Balloon) Squadrons which covered the Birmingham area. For three or four months I worked in the balloon maintenance hangars but, in the middle of this spell, my turn came to act as trailer man on a trip to Widnes to pick up gas for the balloons. Convoys of ten lorries, each towing two trailers loaded with empty gas bottles, made the run at fortnightly intervals. Such trips were regarded as a bit of a scrounge but it didn't turn out that way on this occasion. The trailer man's job was to sit in the back of the lorry and watch the trailers. You are not impressed? I don't blame you. It wasn't until we left the environs of Birmingham and we picked up speed that the fun commenced. Anything over 30 m.p.h the trailers started to snake in opposite directions. At 40 m.p.h the rear trailer could swing from side to side the full width of the road and on descending hills we exceeded this speed very often. Of course, there was little traffic about those days but the roads were narrower, bends were more acute, no banking and often very bumpy. As we roared through villages – no speed limit, of course – the looks on the faces of the locals reflected alarm and dismay. They had no idea what the bottles contained but they looked dangerous and could easily have been mistaken for bombs or torpedoes. This impression was not helped by the fact that someone, humorously, had chalked on the side in large letters BERLIN DIRECT. Onward we surged, snaking our way north, not too worried about the consternation we created but there was little doubt that the operation was VERY DANGEROUS. These days any police patrol would be doing their nut and would have arranged an escort complete with patrol cars fore and aft and motorcycle outriders... all proceeding at a modest pace. Anyway we arrived in Widnes without incident and remained there overnight while the bottles were being filled with hydrogen.

Next morning we took to the road expecting to arrive at Sutton Coldfield at about teatime. We gave little thought to the idea that if we were dangerous yesterday with empty bottles what would the risk be with full bottles? But no one was unduly worried.

The weather had deteriorated and soon it started to snow. The lorries had no ballast over the rear wheels, and even the slightest inclines became increasingly difficult to ascend due to wheel spin. We spent almost the whole day working furiously in a blinding snowstorm shovelling snow and using anything available – sand, gravel, sacks and towing chains – to throw under the wheels in order to maintain traction. By 8 p.m. we reached the outskirts of Whitchurch and were famished, cold and without accommodation, but the local people were very good to us. A number of residents offered beds and food for the night and by 9.30 p.m. we had all been housed and fed... Boy, those tinned sausages and beans tasted good!

Next day we managed only three miles and spent the night on the floor of a pub. The snow had not eased at all and, finally, the following day matters became hopeless. Nearly eighteen inches of snow had fallen in three days. Fortunately, RAF Ternhill was nearby and they had spare accommodation which we gladly accepted. It continued to snow, on and off, for the rest of the week and ten days of heel-kicking monotony elapsed before we were able to proceed back to base.

So, after our little adventure, it was back to work on balloon maintenance... But, not for long... In the first winter of the war enemy air raids were few and far between and in consequence, the expected high load of repair work required on balloons did not materialise. This resulted in spare manpower capacity amongst bods like myself. On the other hand the balloon squadrons were short of manpower so it was no surprise when I was transferred to a Flight Headquarters unit: 913 Squadron situated in a house overlooking Hodgehill Common. Here I was required to provide and account for all equipment and other stores used on the seven balloon sites. Under normal circumstances this job would have been reasonably straightforward but, in wartime conditions, with equipment shortages necessitating urgent movement of items between sites, it was difficult to keep track of some items and inevitably 'paper shortages' occurred. However, it was not long before Birmingham was bombed heavily from time to time. This assisted greatly since any bombs landing on or near a balloon site were a good excuse for writing off specific items of site equipment (apparently) missing and an excellent way of balancing the books.

From our office window overlooking Hodgehill Common it was an exciting sight to see locally produced Spitfire fighters being tested over Castle Bromwich aerodrome, situated some two or three miles away. Their spectacular dives over the airfield followed by breath-taking rolling climbs fired one's imagination. This was the life, I thought, and what I should be trying to achieve. So, when a suitable opportunity occurred I promptly applied for training on air-crew duties and awaited events. Meanwhile, there I was, a miserable balloon rigger/fabric worker misemployed as a storeman. However, because I was not performing the work of my trade and was not officially graded in the stores class, the possibility of promotion was closed to me. In this situation I was obliged to do a smart about turn and 'volunteer' to remuster as an aircrafthand – ACH for short – the lowest form of animal life in the RAF and still, at a lower rate of pay, continue to perform my storeman duties. Unfair? Well per-

935253 ACI Eades, D on guard duties at Hodgehill Common

haps, but as a common 'erk' I could not hope to move the might of the RAF – it would have been easier to attempt to stop the world rotating. For the time being I just had to make the best of it although I was by no means alone in this situation... Another twist in this saga was that having lost my balloon trade I was warned that, in due course, I would become available for posting elsewhere. I was not bothered by this at the time, although I lived to regret it later.

Those were heady days in Birmingham since, despite the reallocation of personnel, we were still short of manpower. Only four of us were available to carry out the basic work... But, in addition to our appointed duties we had to share the manning of the switchboard – open all hours, of course – take turns at dispatch riding and, inevitably, guard duties. These, along with periodic all-night air-raid sessions collectively combined to keep us out of bed as much as possible. At one period the best that one could achieve was a few hours' sleep per week. During a heavy raid one night we heard that distinctive swish of a bomb which we knew must be close by but there was no explosion. Another one for the Air Raid Precaution people to plot we thought. However, shortly after daybreak our neighbour came in to say that there was a hole in his garden at the rear of his patio window and please, could we come and have a look. Two of us went round and one glance was enough... it was an unexploded bomb. Wow... we had spent the night only five yards away and had it detonated, surely we would all have been written off. It did not take us long to evacuate the premises and take all essential gear with us along to the Ward End cricket pavilion. This was a nice place to be on a sunny Saturday afternoon in peacetime, but quite a different proposition during an air raid which occurred the next night. The wooden building shook and reverberated each time the local 3.7 inch anti-aircraft guns and the 4.5 inch battery on the race course opened up, and the effect of falling bombs nearby was dramatic, to say the least. Fortunately, by the next night the bomb disposal squad – stout fellows these, whom I much admired – had removed a 100 lb bomb... just a titchy one they said... and we were then able to move back to our office.

About a fortnight later a raid was in progress and a balloon site required some essential equipment. Site 67 was situated farthest away from Hodgehill Common – Sod's Law again – but there was no alternative, we would have to deliver. Les, the driver, helped me to load the lorry and off we went. We could see the glow in the sky that the raid was concentrated in the direction we were heading and, apart from anything else, we would have to watch for bomb craters in the road. The streets were deserted – no traffic, no people, not even a stray cat – it was eerie. As we progressed, the glow in the sky turned to raw flames leaping high and illuminating the smoke which was billowing up in great cumulus clouds. The horizon flickered constantly with Ack-Ack gun fire and the sky sparkled with the explosion of bursting shells, as we approached Adderley Park balloon site. We could see that on the opposite side the Ty-Phoo tea factory was on fire from end to end and that searchlights were very active.

We alighted from the lorry and were met by the site corporal. Our greetings were cordial and we spoke for a moment or two as though everything was normal. Then suddenly... whoosh... kerrump, a flash from a bomb bursting half a mile away made us jump – then another this time nearer... Jees... the three of us made a concerted dive under the lorry. I started to count – three – four – five – six then silence... Phew! I had broken out in a sweat... so had the others. We did not linger. The stores were off-loaded, signed for, and we retreated smartly. On the way back we spotted a lot of damage and had difficulty in dodging piles of rubble, and sometimes glass, here and there. As we turned into Flight HQ the Commanding Officer – F/Lt Hawkes – and others were keen to know how much damage we had seen and where. I felt sorry for them. Many were older local chaps who had joined the Auxiliary Air Force pre-war and had been called up in August 1939. Some were naturally worried about the welfare of their families and friends and we were very closely questioned.

A few nights later I suffered the indignity of being blown off my motorcycle when attempting to deliver a message to the balloon site on the Birmingham race course. Fortunately, it was one of the Hun's smaller bombs but it was near enough to me to feel a hot blast run up my trouser leg and out of my collar. You don't believe me? I don't blame you – neither did my mates. They thought I had gone to sleep in the saddle and dreamt it... I was very short of sleep, we all were, but I assure you that's the way it was.

Later the same night Les – our transport driver – and two other colleagues had gone down to a local fish and chip shop but had not returned as expected. Slowly, news filtered through that the shop had been demolished by a landmine and that all three men had perished. This was shattering news but as ever, in wartime, our work carried on as normal... Next day it was a poignant sight to see the battered remains of their little Austin 7 tourer with its distinctive pea green wire-spoked wheels lying upside down on a heap of rubble, which marked the spot of a once-busy suburban shopping centre. One victim was a local chap – our flight mechanic – and we attended his funeral three days later. It was a very sad occasion for all of us.

The operation of the telephone switchboard was an interesting job, because it was the main source of operational control. All balloon sites were linked to the 'box' and, by depressing seven keys, they could all receive information or instructions at the same time. The drill was simple. As soon as all seven 'lights'* indicated readiness to receive messages were given and, at the end, each site acknowledged by giving its site number in numerical sequence. It was important that operational information should be relayed quickly and this arrangement was as speedy as could be devised... From HQ we received warnings of air raids: Yellow, standy-by; Red, immediate action. Orders to fly balloons and at what height, or conversely to bed down... Weather forecasts – secret in wartime – were relayed in code. Information about wind direction and speeds, cloud amounts and particularly the degree of thunder risks were essential to those manning the balloon sites. Normally barrages were raised before dusk and bedded down for daily inspection after dawn but they had to be ready to fly at any time. Occasionally, the Luftwaffe would send over the odd bomber or two in daylight when the cloud base was low and the thunder risk high. In such cases it would have been disastrous to have flown the entire barrage so, instead, only two balloons per flight would fly at cloud base. I remember this happening twice in Birmingham. Orders were given to fly and we went outside to see the results. The effect of electrical discharges was spectacular, but we were not pleased to see the balloons bows' turn from silver to cherry red and then burst into flames and cascade to the ground at £500 a time. Balloons were very susceptible to static electricity, even in good weather conditions, and although the winch vehicles were well earthed, to avoid receiving shocks, balloon crews always jumped on and off.

One night a red alert was in force but Birmingham was not the target. Instead bombers droned wm-wm-wm overhead about one every ten minutes in a northerly direction probably making for Liverpool or Manchester. I was sitting in the office when suddenly there was a yelp from the telephone operator... Flushed and excited he

---

* silver hemispheroids.

looked over his shoulder and shouted 'I've got Cromwell'. Blimey! We had a quick look at the code book and there it was ... Paratroops landing ... Seven keys on the switchboard went down smartly and I dashed off to inform the flight commander, who immediately issued orders for us to man the sand-bagged trench, which had been prepared on Hodgehill Common. Bods were dashing about in all directions collecting their gear but it was not long before we were all assembled in the trench complete with tin hats, gas capes, rifles and ammunition. It was a cool, clear, still night and we could easily hear orders being shouted to the crews on the 3.7 inch gun site over a mile away ... The position of the trench had been well chosen and we had an uninterrupted view over a wide area. There was sufficient light for us to see all round and we watched and waited it seemed for hours until eventually a runner – who had been left behind along with the 'teleop' and guard – came with the news that we could stand down. What a relief, but we had lost the best part of a night's sleep ... yet again.

My posting elsewhere which had been pending arrived when least expected and turned out to be RAF Aldergrove in Northern Ireland. This was a blow ... In a strange way I had grown quite attached to the flight and its personnel. Good camaraderie existed and we had been through some pretty rough times together. But, more importantly, Northern Ireland was just about the last place I wished to go to on a home posting anyway, because letter censorship operated and leave was restricted to and taken at six-monthly intervals on a rota basis. There was no possibility of occasional short or long weekend breaks hitch-hiking home which was very regrettable, since Chic and I had been married only some months previously.

Before leaving Birmingham I was called to an aircrew selection board. I, along with a few others from No 5 Balloon Centre, had been well primed about these boards. I knew, for certain, that I was educationally and physically suitable, but would I be able to convince the board that I possessed the other necessary qualities such as aptitude, alertness and tenacity? Could my resolution be revealed without seeming downright aggressive? Not an easy thing for a Geordie to do. In the waiting room we sat around in little groups making desultory comments and waiting uneasily to be called for interview. At last, the fateful moment arrived and I made my formal entrance into a well-appointed room. To my surprise the board consisted of one squadron leader who immediately put me at ease with simple questions and the interview seemed to be developing into a cosy chat. Going the wrong way, I thought. I had had no chance to demonstrate my keenness and penetration and there was no way of turning the conversation to the points I had rehearsed so carefully beforehand. Suddenly, the vital question was put. 'Do you wish to wait for a pilot's course or would you rather train as an air gunner now?' How does one answer this question without knowing the statistical facts behind the scene? In the main, each applicant wished to be a pilot, of course, but how oversubscribed were they? If I said I would wait, would this be regarded as a lack of keenness to fly? (We had been warned of this possible pitfall.) I had to say something quickly and almost involuntarily I replied, 'Sir, I wish to be trained as an air gunner now.' With a smile the squadron leader, no doubt feeling that he had manoeuvred me exactly into the position he wanted, nodded and indicated that matters would proceed from there. So bang went my dreams of flinging a Spitfire about the sky. Perhaps if I had called his bluff (if it was) I might now be telling a different story, or perhaps, none at all.

Chapter 3

Taking a Chance Light-ly

Have you ever seen passengers leaning over a ship's rail being sick? I have – it's quite remarkable really – as the vessel ploughs through the waves into a stiff breeze, the contents of someone's stomach flies horizontally backwards and if one is nearer to the stern quick evasive action is essential. I learnt this on a rough crossing from Stranraer to Larne.

I made the crossing by ferry to Northern Ireland and took a train to Belfast. Sitting on my kit bag, in a corner of the main railway station awaiting transport to RAF Aldergrove, I spotted a large poster which invited the world to COME TO ULSTER. However, somebody with a typically British sense of humour had scrawled underneath in large capitals AND BRING YOUR RAINCOAT AND GUMBOOTS. At the time I regarded this comment as friendly leg pull but I had plenty of chances later to appreciate the more serious implication.

Aldergrove is pleasantly situated on the shores of Lough Neagh not far from Antrim. It proved to be a good station. The food was certainly more plentiful and varied than I had become accustomed to in Birmingham and our hut was warm and comfortable. This might have had something to do with the fact that the airman in charge of issuing the daily coal ration lived in Hut 54 – our hut. Within the perimeter of the camp there was a Sandes Home which provided tasty food, at reasonable cost, and had recreational facilities. The latter were important, since at off-duty times there was nothing to do in the surrounding district and airmen were not encouraged to visit Belfast, where 'tarring and feathering' of personnel was not unknown. Or so it was said. Presumably pre-war Aldergrove had little night-flying activity. It probably possessed a petrol driven generator coupled to a floodlight – known as a Chance Light – which could be used to illuminate a portion of the drome. This would be supplemented by parallel lines of gooseneck oil flares suitable for landing small light aircraft. However, under wartime operational conditions better take-off and landing facilities for Coastal Command's 206 Squadron were an obvious requirement. Their Hudson aircraft laden with fuel and depth charges for hunting German submarines in the Atlantic and their relatively high landing speeds needed runway lights over at least 2,000 yards. Pending the installation of a permanent lighting system, temporary measures had been taken to provide this requirement. Surplus five-gallon oil drums had been cunningly converted to hold and protect electric lights. These lined the runway at about 30-yard intervals and were linked to the generator in one huge DC circuit. The generator also supplied power to the Chance Light on a separate circuit.

I was assigned to a squad of three, known as 'flare path wallahs' and it was our job to operate the equipment... Each afternoon the flare path had to be laid out and, of course, taken in each morning. It was quite a sight to see our equipment being transported to and fro. After the tractor came the Chance Light and generator unit, then two flat trailers containing the flare path lights, followed by another full of goose-neck flares and finally an object which could be opened into the form of a T to indicate the wind direction to pilots. The appearance of this miscellaneous outfit – all of 20 yards long – with its crew hanging on precariously, always raised smiles and (ignoring crudity) whimsical comments from onlookers. Nevertheless, this equipment, Heath Robinsonish as it was, had a serious function to perform. It took quite a time to lay out the runway lights and care had to be taken since a loose connection, or indeed a broken bulb, meant no light anywhere... However, eventually, with the runway lights linked up to the generator satisfactorily and the Chance Lights working, we were ready to receive an incoming aircraft. But, then came the tricky bit... A plane usually landed on the floodlit runway abreast of the Chance Light but, after the first 50 yards, the pilot began to run into his own shadow – much to his bewilderment. The drill therefore was for the Chance Light to be switched off at this point. That was fine but if this were to be done the whole of the generator's load would be diverted to the runway circuit and the lights would blow... To overcome this problem it was necessary to switch off both the Chance Light *and* the runway lights, while adjustments were made after which the runway lights could be restored.* The snag here was that the pilot had no lights at all for about two or three seconds... Can you imagine his feeling when suddenly changing from glaring light to nothing and blinding down the runway at 90 m.p.h in total darkness hoping that the generator operator – at which we took turns – didn't boob... I fear that pilots of Hudson aircraft must have suffered some anxious moments although amazingly during the time I was on runway duties no accident occurred due to inadequate, if not downright dangerous, night-landing equipment.

One night a Hudson lined up to take off for a 'circuits and bumps' session. The green light given, all seemed well as it trundled up the runway but, just at the point where the pilot would be easing back the 'stick', the aircraft's nose rose almost vertically into the air. With engines thrashing and straining at full blast, the plane climbed to 200 feet then stalled and, to our horror, fell sideways to strike the ground on wing-tip and tailplane. It immediately burst into flames... The emergency services were quickly on the scene but nothing could be done. Miraculously one of the crew survived, but two perished in the flames. We were all very grieved about this incident.

The Meteorological Flight pilots commanded our respect and admiration. Obviously the collection of data for weather forecasting purposes was of vital importance to the RAF particularly and the other services generally. The Met Flight had a reputation of flying in any weather come what may, and had not been known to back down even in the face of frightful odds against. On one Sunday, snow had been falling thickly and continuously for a long period and at about

---

* The drill was to switch off the Chance Light and runway lights; furiously wind back a variable resistance and then switch on the runway lights. Sounds easy but the awkward position of the switches and resistance made for difficulties. Darkness and inclement weather didn't help either.

2 p.m. we were called out to lay and light the goose-neck oil flares on the runway. The snow was so thick it took a considerable time to find the runway but, after much probing, we managed to mark out a strip about 100 yards long and line it with flares. The old Gloster Gladiator biplane could now take off as usual on its daily flight, although the visibility could not have been more than 30 yards. While take off was achieved with little difficulty, the problem of landing again without modern blind-flying aids was another matter... Usually these flights, which obtained data at altitude over base, took a little less than an hour to complete and we waited, somewhat anxiously, in the lee of a snow wall we had built for the return of the Gladiator. In due course we heard the plane circling above the drome, obviously the pilot was in some difficulty. Five minutes passed and the droning continued on and off – then silence. Oh God, what had happened? We looked at each other fearing the worst, when suddenly we heard the roar of an engine combined with the familiar whine of an approaching aircraft and then, just above the beginning of the runway, the Gladiator appeared. The pilot made a perfect landing. None of us, including the duty pilot, knew how he had managed to find the landing point in an absolute white-out. The only thing in his favour was that the intensity of the snow had eased just a little, momentarily, and perhaps he had followed this gap and through it had recognised some local landmark, which enabled him to line up with the runway... but this is pure conjecture. I never knew the name of the pilot but he was obviously a brave and very capable fellow.

Going on leave from Aldergrove was a tedious business involving transport to Belfast, train to Larne and ferry to Stranraer, followed by a long train journey changing at Carlisle and Newcastle. The better way was to hitch a lift on any aircraft leaving for the mainland and, in this respect, the occupants of Hut 54 were again fortunate, since one of our number, called Hutch, worked in the control tower and was able to fix things with the Flight Controller. So, twice I was able to hitch flights, to Leuchars in Fife, and to Netheravon in Wiltshire. Although both these places were a long way from Sunderland, I still managed to arrive home well in advance of the time it would have taken travelling by the regular route. It was between these leaves that my little daughter was born and she would be three months old before I would see her. I had this to look forward to, but an unforeseen event was to play its part.

A huge consignment of 100 octane fuel in four-gallon drums had arrived at Aldergrove. These were to be opened and emptied into bowsers (mobile petrol tanks), and this extraneous job was allotted to the flarepath wallahs. Fork-lift trucks were not available those days and not even a porter's barrow could be obtained, so the drums, which were very heavy, had to be carried by hand two at a time, over some distance. After a few weeks of this laborious and repetitive work I developed a hernia in my right groin . . . I was suddenly faced with a problem. My second leave was due shortly and I did not wish to report sick and enter a hospital in Northern Ireland which, apart from anything else, would have jeopardised my leave. Alternatively, I could not declare my dilemma and thereby dodge out of heavy work which could aggravate my injury even to the point of strangulation . . . What was I to do? Take a chance lightly – like a pilot speeding down the runway without lights – not knowing quite where he was going or what the outcome would be? After much cogitation I decided that this was the way it had to be, and I would try to keep my head down and avoid trouble as much as possible, until it was time to go on leave. Luckily, I managed to get by without further damage to my injury.

There was much celebration when I finally arrived home to hold my baby daughter for the first time. One of the never to be forgotten, pleasurable moments in my life, of which Chic and I were very proud.

My leave was nearly over and I consulted our family doctor who confirmed that I had a rupture and advised me to report to a local military unit. There the young medical officer, having diagnosed a bubonocele, somewhat apologetically advised me that I would need an operation and that I must not return to my unit until this was performed. I am sure my face was solemn and worried looking, but inwardly I was smiling. The operation, which had been pending for weeks would now be performed locally and I would be able to see my wife and daughter over an extended period. Actually things worked out much better than I could possibly have expected . . . The local military hospital had a fair quota of Royal Artillery personnel requiring hernia operations. Moving heavy shells and loading guns had taken its toll amongst the gun crews and, worse still, some gunners had been returning to duty after their operations too soon, with consequent disastrous results. The local rule was, therefore, that each soldier must remain in bed for a period of 28 days after his operation and thereafter must proceed to a convalescent centre for a period of four weeks and, in true military fashion, what applied to gunners would also apply to all other service personnel. This suited me very well and was better than anything I could have planned on my own. After my operation and the regular period in bed I, along with a mixed squad of chaps all dressed in hospital blue, was dispatched to a home at Lartington near Barnard Castle in County Durham. The commandant was an excellent Red Cross lady who had converted her home into a convalescent centre for the duration of the war. We were looked after very well in comfortable surroundings. Our daily sessions with the physiotherapist, medicine ball and football were enjoyable and literally just what the doctor ordered. Better still, I was able to find digs locally for Chic and Valerie and, as we were free each afternoon, I was able to spend many happy hours with them. It was summertime, the weather was good and we all enjoyed what amounted to the first real holiday break since the beginning of the war.

From time to time I wondered about what had happened to my training as an air gunner. The result of my board had been confirmed in writing but I had expected to be called much earlier. Inquiries I had made produced no positive or worthwhile news so there was nothing I could do other than let the administrative machinery grind on in the knowledge that sometime it would all happen. Meanwhile, just at this period it would not really matter, since obviously training could not start until I was confirmed as medically fit.

Following Lartington I had a fortnight's convalescent leave but the day inevitably arrived for me to return to Northern Ireland. I knew I would have some difficulty in travelling since I possessed only a leave pass which was about 10 weeks out-of-date and a sealed foolscap envelope marked MEDICAL DOCUMENTS – CONFIDENTIAL. Sure enough, the military police at Newcastle Central Station regarded my out-of-date pass with great suspicion and it was not long before I was marched into their office for quizzing by their sergeant. He obviously thought my story was rather thin. The medical documents could have proved that what I was saying was correct but he had no authority to open them, so he was in a bit of a quandary. I, of course, was not in the least concerned about his dilemma and could sense his annoyance, but after some muttering and, in view of the fact that the boat train was due to leave, he reluctantly indicated that I could go but, no doubt, my movements would be carefully watched... However, I had no further difficulties during the rest of my journey back to Aldergrove, where I received a cheer from my Hut 54 colleagues – 'Where've yer been... thought you'd done a bunk over the border... lost your memory I suppose' were typical comments even if I have been censorial in not recording the derogatory terms one airman customarily used when speaking to another. They were a good lot of chaps. The huts contained thirty or forty airmen in fairly crowded conditions. The beds were arranged in a way that allowed eight feet of space between each head when sleeping top-to-tail (as it were) – a medical officer's requirement. A good percentage of the occupants were from Eire or Northern Ireland and of mixed religions, but generally a harmonious atmosphere prevailed and any rows breaking out were not between the Irish elements but the remainder, which mainly comprised Englishmen. I remember one brawny chap from Sheffield, who had been provoked by his neighbour, suddenly bawling out in his broad Yorkshire dialect 'arl 'it thee reet 'tween peepers'. He could and would have but the entire occupants of the hut fell about with laughter and he turned away remarking with a grin, 'Next time.'

Some weeks after I returned to Aldergrove I was told to report to the Aircrew Receiving Centre (ACRC) in St John's Wood, London. My heart leapt... at last things were happening, as the cobbler might have observed. I spent little time going round the usual sections collecting signatures on my clearance certificate. Funny, I thought, how systematic the RAF was in making sure that before anyone left the station all steps were taken to ensure the return of any equipment on charge and recoup any money owing. In other words the pound of flesh was always demanded and obtained, but no reciprocity had been built into the system to protect the interests of the individual.

I packed my kit-bag and left Hut 54 having received the good wishes of my friends, but in their eyes I was definitely a lucky bastard to have obtained a posting back to the mainland... Whatever, my course was set for London.

At ACRC time was spent either attending parades or being medically examined. The main assembly point was situated outside but sometimes inside Lord's Cricket Ground, which provided a point of interest to those like myself, who were attracted to the game. One couldn't help wondering how many years would pass before a world torn by strife and destruction could return to normal and the sound of bat on ball would be heard again at Cricket HQ. One could only dream but, meanwhile, the hard facts of life of medical examinations had to be faced. These were very thorough and long drawn out affairs. Eyes, ears and teeth came under very critical examination but heart, respiration, blood pressure, balance, reflexes and, seemingly, most bodily functions were tested in some way. We were prodded, poked, hammered, bent over and much of our time was spent starkers or near so. All necessary, I suppose, in view of the stresses and strains we would be subject to in due course. Eventually the thumbs-up sign was given and posting instructions were awaited.

Chapter 4

Initial Training

There is, as I was to discover, much more to air gunnery than would appear on the surface. One might assume that it is a simple matter when sitting in a turret to point a pair of guns at a target, press the button and BINGO, bits of an attacking aircraft would fly off in all directions. Not a bit of it – firing a weapon when stationary on the ground at a ground target with only wind and gravity to consider is one thing. Firing, stationary on the ground at a moving target in the air is another and a more complicated matter, involving something called deflection.* But firing when in motion at a target, which is also moving, is a complex problem, except in certain conditions when opposing factors cancel each other out. The science of aiming, or the theory of sighting, is a subject on its own and would need a chapter to explain in any sort of depth, but broadly the accuracy and therefore success of air gunners depends on being able to gauge the distance of an attacking fighter and to determine its angle and line of approach.

On the mechanical and practical side it was necessary to learn a good deal about machine guns, cannons and hydraulically or electrically operated turret systems. Was so much knowledge really necessary? Well, air gunners were completely responsible for the maintenance of their guns and did not rely, in any way, on the services of an armourer. A good thing too, since if guns did not fire at the vital

---

* Distance moved by a target during time of flight of the bullet.

moment there could be no recriminations. Knowledge of the various turret systems was not so essential since the chance of being able to rectify anything other than simple faults in flight, especially in the dark and sub-zero temperatures at 20,000 feet, was questionable. Nevertheless, each gunner possessed a sound knowledge of his equipment and could carry out certain remedial work should the occasion arise. All this was in line with service training which was devoted to producing proficient operational units. RAF crews were self-reliant and capable of navigating to and bombing any target within range, unlike our American counterparts who tended to fly in massive formations on a follow-my-leader basis for navigation and bombing. Their personnel seemed to know little about the workings of their equipment. However this is, by no means, a criticism of their efforts. They did an excellent job in their own way and took their fair share of the load, resultant honours and heavy losses.

My initial practical training was received, in the autumn of 1942, at RAF Credenhill near Hereford. Basically, this was a school for armourers but a shortened course had been introduced for air gunners. The pressure was intense at this highly disciplined school. The less formal life of the wartime RAF had not reached this unit. It was still operating the peacetime 'bull' routine, but the overall syllabus time must have been severely curtailed, which resulted in long concentrated lectures. Even break times were organised and supervised. Ten minutes was allowed for the march to the NAAFI canteen and to stand in the queue for a 'char and large wad', five minutes to consume same, followed immediately by fifteen minutes concentrated physical training. How our digestive systems stood up to this treatment, heaven knows, but many of us always returned to the lecture room burping loudly. The course, if highly condensed, was interesting and within the scope of those willing to concentrate fully, as most of us were. Although there was so much to learn, no relaxation in domestic cleaning of billets and presentation of equipment for inspection was tolerated. After one inspection we were told that, because of some triviality, all members of the hut including the corporals, would have to report to the cookhouse for 'fatigues'. Clearly, this was a very unfair and indiscriminate penalty and we decided en masse that we would disregard the instruction. Fortunately, there must have been a breakdown in communications between the station warrant officer's office and those in charge of the cookhouse, since we heard nothing further. We were lucky to get away with our mutinous conduct...

On Sundays the church parade always ended with a march past the saluting base on the square which faced in a westerly direction. One Sunday the weather seemed reasonable and therefore no order was given for greatcoats to be worn. We were lined up as usual for the march past and we could see in the valley to the west that a huge deluge was threatening to burst over the camp, but no steps were taken to cancel the parade. As we marched, the storm drew nearer and, with impeccable timing just before we reached the saluting base, it broke. The order 'eyes right' was given and with a smart turn of the head there before us was the sight of the commanding officer and his entourage at the salute, facing torrential rain, gritting their teeth and rapidly becoming drenched through. Having left the base we were rapidly dismissed but there was still at least half the parade yet to pay their respects. We were certainly wet, but those in command must have felt as though they had been dragged through Niagara Falls and would not be amused over the incident. We, on the other hand, felt elated.

Perhaps I have been rather scathing about the harsh discipline at this establishment, but it was only the administration that was the problem. The instructors were very excellent chaps who did their very best to ensure that we obtained full benefit from the course. I think they were pleased with the examination results which showed they had done their job well in teaching us to handle and maintain various guns and other weapons, and in imparting essential knowledge about turret systems, turret components and sundry pyrotechnics concerned with aircraft... Anyway, with examinations over, a batch of us were assigned to No 2 Air Gunners' School at Dalcross... Dalcross? Where's that? A quick look on the map revealed that it was situated in north-west Scotland on the Moray Firth not far from Inverness... Hereford to Inverness in December on a long overnight train journey. We now began to realise the reason for the RAF's motto *per ardua ad astra*.

Chapter 5

Coloured Holes Count

'Get yer feet off the deck' was an oft used saying in the RAF and at Dalcross they quickly gave it credence. I was surprised at the celerity with which I found myself in the air... Whoosh... The 'there I was' situation came home to me... three thousand feet up, sitting alone in a gun turret with the sky and mountains changing places and spinning one way and then the other as the pilot practised slow rolls. His repertoire seemed endless – loops and dives followed by steep climbing turns demonstrated the power of G forces and the helplessness it creates. Ten minutes of aerobatics mixed with the inhalation of exhaust fumes made me feel quite queasy and I was in no position after landing to return the wave of an excited young chap who was running along with us on the other side of the chain-link perimeter fence. His faith in the impregnability of the RAF must have been shaken that day but, at least, I wasn't sick in the turret!

This was an enlightening experience with which to commence my training as air gunner at Dalcross. Defiant aircraft were flown, in the main, by Polish pilots who had a great sense of fun and were full of *joie de vivre* but we soon became used to their outlandish routine. The Defiant was an interesting plane. It had been introduced in the late 1930s and had received a lot of publicity. The Defiant was a fighter, but it was unique and quite unlike the Spitfire or Hurricane. It was a two seater – pilot and gunner – the latter in an electronically operated Boulton Paul turret mounted aft of the cockpit. During the

THE TURRETS OF WAR

A Defiant fighter plane with Boulton Paul gun turret

Course 39 – RAF Dalcross

evacuation of Dunkirk the Defiants had a brief moment of glory. In the Battle of Britain, 141 and 264 Squadrons were equipped with Defiants, but they were badly mauled by the German Me 109 fighters – the main disadvantage was the heaviness of the turret and because of this the planes were being used in situations beyond their capabilities. However, they achieved limited success as a night-fighter, being used by about a dozen squadrons. At that time airborne interception was in its infancy but, nevertheless, 256 Squadron recorded seven confirmed 'kills' and four probables during the Blitz of 1940–41. However, on being withdrawn from operations the aircraft were pressed into service for air gunnery training.

There were thirteen (!) trainees on Course 39 (3 × 13!) and the flying schedule was very tight due, presumably, to the fact that in mid-winter the amount of daylight in the north of Scotland is much reduced. However, air-firing sorties were well controlled and we were able to complete the scheduled programme on time, even if one had to scamper about between trips – not always easy when encumbered with flying clothing and other paraphernalia. For safety purposes there was a strict drill in the turret for both take off and landing and with this completed, the pilot was free to proceed. Flying over the Moray Firth contact was made with a drogue-towing Lysander aircraft. The drogue target – a conical canvas sleeve open at both ends – trailed about 400 yards behind the Lysander and with both aircraft flying at even speed, straightforward firing at it on the beam (ie at 90 degrees to the line of flight) allowing only for deflection was relatively easy. The earlier exercises were good fun. However, they became more difficult when relative speeds and distance apart of the two aircraft varied, for which due allowances had to be made. The ammunition used had been dipped in slow-drying coloured paint. On landing the coloured holes were counted and identified with the appropriate gunner and from this information the percentage of hits could be calculated. A score of five per cent was considered satisfactory but, with all due modesty, I usually managed to beat this and even scored eighteen per cent on one occasion, although I suspect that someone had miscalculated. Later in the course, guns were replaced by cine-cameras. For these exercises Defiants would take off in pairs and pilots took turns in making mock attacks on each other while gunners took turns in 'firing' at the attacker. The results of these cine-films, although somewhat jumpy, could be plotted and assessed with some accuracy. There is no doubt, in my mind, that these exercises were of greater value than live firing of guns at a drogue. They simulated all the fighting manoeuvres one would expect to experience and were as near to actual combat conditions as could be devised.

One day on returning from such an exercise, when his plane was upside down, an unfortunate gunner slipped from his safety belt and slid into the space between the guns and the top of the turret... Unluckily for him he became well and truly stuck in that position when he accidentally tripped the gas bottle and inflated his Mae West (life jacket). He was not able to warn the pilot of his plight and, not being able to move, the subsequent landing must have been a painful process. No doubt the ground crew enjoyed the experience of releasing him from his predicament, and offered him worldly advice on how to prevent a repeat performance... Life was never dull at No 2 AGS Dalcross.

Flying exercises were interspersed with classroom work on tactics and manoeuvres, general safety procedures, parachute drill, gunnery and sighting theory. As an adjunct to the latter, time was spent on skeet (clay pigeon) shooting with 12-bore guns. This was an invaluable exercise since one quickly learnt to aim behind the skeet, then pull the gun through the line of flight to a point ahead and fire. The success or otherwise of one's endeavours depended on whether the correct line had been followed and if the appropriate amount of deflection had been allowed. It was all very concentrated stuff but fortunately we had a small break in the middle of it, when Christmas Day arrived. I must say that everything was done to forget the war, food shortages and general troubles. We enjoyed the traditional dinner served by the officers and sergeants. It was a good show and, being north of the border, we hoped that it would be repeated at Hogmanay, but no such luck. However, we did have a cross-country run. I used to enjoy these outings especially when the course was over rough country and through partially snow-covered pine woods. I did expect to play football but was disappointed – in Scotland, and no football on New Year's Day? We deserved to lose the war!

Having absorbed all the theory; after banging off 3,000 rounds of ammunition – there must be millions of spent rounds in the Moray

Firth – and 100 feet of cine-film in the air, we were adjudged sufficiently trained to proceed to the next stage elsewhere. So, at a short ceremony, our big moment had come. We were presented with our air gunner's badges – half wings – and sergeants' chevrons by the chief training officer and sent on our way.

Some of us were posted to RAF Lindholme, near Doncaster. We hastily packed our two kit-bags, threw them aboard a lorry and headed for Inverness. In the little time we had to spare we sauntered up Castle Street to view the scene from the top ... A worthwhile vista of this beautifully laid out burgh, over which Flora Macdonald gazes reflectively in the direction of the Isle of Skye. However we could not linger too long since ahead lay another long 15-hour journey from 3 p.m. to 6 a.m. the next day – in total darkness for most of the time.

Chapter 6

Circuits and Bumps

Crews manning operational squadrons in Bomber and Coastal Command included air gunners. Both Commands were equipped with heavy aircraft fitted with gun turrets and it was a gunner's job to defend them from attack by enemy fighters. I had been chosen for Bomber Command and would be flying in a Lancaster bomber. Three gun turrets were installed in this aircraft: one at the front normally manned by the bomb aimer: one at the rear manned, obviously, by the rear gunner, or tail-end Charlie as he was often known, and finally the mid-upper position, which I would be occupying.

Lancaster bombers were not large aircraft by today's standard. Nothing like the size of a DC 10 or a Jumbo Jet 747, for example. Nevertheless, we regarded them as large for their time, more than fifty years ago. They were powered by four Rolls-Royce Merlin engines and had a wing span of just over 100 feet and a length of nearly 70 feet. The all-up weight was a little short of 30 tons. The bomb load varied according to distance of the target – more fuel, fewer bombs and vice versa – but probably averaged 8,000 pounds of mixed explosive and incendiary bombs per raid. The maximum speed was 266 m.p.h. but the cruising speed was about 216 m.p.h. and they could fly up to 25,000 feet. The overall armament consisted of 8 Browning machine guns.

It was early February 1943 and our little group of gunners from Dalcross arrived at RAF Lindholme tired, cold and dispirited. But after a warm breakfast, we all perked up at the news that we would be meeting our crews later in the morning.

The crew I would be joining had been together for some weeks at an Operational Training Unit (OTU), gaining experience on a twin-engined Wellington aircraft. The time had come for the pilot to convert to four-engined craft and this he would do at Lindholme – 1656 Conversion Unit.

We were all assembled in a large room and, after some preliminary announcements about the training programme, our names were read out alongside the names of the pilots. I had been allocated to Sgt Wells. By trial and error we eventually managed to find each other and I was introduced to the rest of the crew. They were all sergeants with the exception of the wireless operator who was a pilot officer. For the next few months my mates would be:

MAURICE WELLS. Pilot. Aged 24, a civil engineer from Christchurch, New Zealand. Tall, erect, prematurely bald – but it suited him – gentle, tended to be shy, quiet and unassuming.

JOE GALLOWAY. Navigator. Aged 23, a ginger-haired Geordie from Darlington who had previously worked in the architect's department of the local authority.

TREVOR GIRDLESTONE. Wireless Operator. Aged 22, a tall good-looking Rhodesian who had failed a pilot's course but was nevertheless competent at the controls. A useful man to have in the crew should anything untoward happen to the skipper.

TOMMY MOORE. Bomb Aimer. Aged 19, a quiet happy chap from Leicester who joined the RAF direct from school. He derived fame from an incident during his earlier training when the crew had to land unexpectedly on the Isle of Man. He had no shoes with him but insisted on going to a local dance wearing clumpy flying boots. As he ploughed around the floor he rapidly became referred to as Puss in Boots and the nickname stuck to him for a time.

HARRY MORETON. Flight Engineer. Aged 21, a quiet and friendly engine fitter from Blackpool who possessed a homely Lancashire dialect. Completely unflappable.

RAY TERRY. Rear Gunner. Aged 22, another good-looking Rhodesian. Voluble and extrovert.

Without knowing the crew members you might regard them as just a random collection of airmen with no special attributes but, in fact, each possessed unique skills plus a very sober and objective approach to the job to be done. Openly we would be quite cynical about each other's performance, but this was only superficial boyishness. In fact, a bond of friendly trust and respect existed, which made for easy working relationships.

The training of the Conversion Unit was mainly for the benefit of the pilot and flight engineer. The flying involved what seemed to be endless hours of 'circuits and bumps' – up, round and down again, continuously. All very necessary, but deadly boring for the rest of the crew who had to sit there and endure. On occasions, however, the monotony was relieved by gun firing and practice bombing trips.

However, all this gave me the opportunity to accustom myself to the mid-upper turret. It was completely different from the Defiant's turret, especially in the controls, which was a welcome improvement. I was impressed by this, but even more so by the almost uninterrupted all-round view one obtained perched high up amidships. When facing aft there was sufficient metalwork to afford some protection and conveniently placed ammunition cans on each side made good arm rests. An important feature was an inbuilt protection device which prevented one from shooting at vital sections of the aircraft. After all, being amidships I could see nearly all parts on the top of the plane and, without the protection, in the heat of battle, would be able to shoot at the tail assembly, wings, engines, and indeed every member of the crew – excluding self, of course. I was pleased about this... so were the crew.

Of the three gun turret positions on a Lancaster bomber the front unit could be generally discounted for night-fighter defence purposes since frontal attacks, except over the target, were rare. This meant that only the rear and mid-upper turrets were effectively in contention. The rear gunner could rotate his turret through 180 degrees from beam to beam and had clear visibility above and level, but was somewhat restricted below. The mid-upper could rotate through 360 degrees with excellent visibility above and level but restricted below, except on either beam aft of the wings and forward of the tailplane. The hydraulically operated turrets were immediately responsive to the controls. In action, the guns could quickly be brought to bear

THE TURRETS OF WAR

A Lancaster bomber U-Uncle of 12 Squadron

A Fraser Nash rear gun turret on Lancaster bomber

on the target and the speed then regulated with ease to follow any desired line smoothly. The gun sight was a most efficient piece of equipment. Through a hooded reflection panel it superimposed an illuminated ring and centre dot (a graticule) on the attacking fighter, at the fighter's range (thus eliminating parallax error). This was important since the radius of the ring was used to determine the distance of the target, a factor which had to be taken into account since the fighting range was 400 yards for both fighter and bomber.

The latter's guns were harmonised (preadjusted) to allow for gravity drop and fire into an area 4 feet 6 inches square at this distance. The sight also assisted in calculating the amount of deflection to allow for the distance moved by the target during the time of flight of the bullet. It also would indicate the line on which deflection should be laid.

The mid-upper turret was ideally situated to observe the Drem night landing system in action at Lindholme. The outer circuit of the drome was well marked with white lights leading into a funnel approach to the landing end of the runway, which was similarly marked on both sides of its full length. At the beginning of the runway, at each side, a steady coloured light indicated to the pilot how accurate his approach angle and height was. Thus: yellow, too high; green, correct; red, too low. So by maintaining a steady green light the pilot would arrive over the central part of the runway at the correct height. If his height was correct but his position relative to the centre of the runway was too much to one side the steady green light would change to long flashes (dashes) or if the other side short flashes (dots). This simple system was very effective and helpful to pilots, but I couldn't help thinking how sophisticated it was compared with the ghastly equipment in use at Aldergrove which, in comparison, was apparatus more appropriate to the Stone Age. To be fair, of course, it was a matter of priority. Lindholme by its very nature had to cope with almost continuous night-flying sessions whereas at Aldergrove night landings were relatively few. Incidentally, a modified and more accurate Drem system is still used at airports today. Apart from having no left-right indicators its basic principles are the same.

Those early training days enabled me to get to know my colleagues and to learn more about their jobs. The skipper's job and that of Joe the navigator, also Terry the rear gunner, were obvious but what did Harry do as a flight engineer? In many ways he was the skipper's right-hand man – he assisted with the engine controls on take off and landing, also operating the flaps and undercarriage; he monitored the engines' performance to achieve economic running and changed fuel tanks as necessary; had control of and monitored oxygen supplies and could release bombs manually – in case of a hang-up – but more about this later. Obviously Tommy's chief job was to drop the bomb

CIRCUITS AND BUMPS

load on the target but, in addition, he acted as front gunner and assisted the navigator by map reading and pinpointing our position as required. He was in fact a qualified navigator and could have taken over the job in the event of an emergency. This leaves Trevor, the wireless operator. Needless to say his main job was to transmit and receive messages but in addition he was a trained gunner and could man a turret if necessary. He was also in charge of the pigeons... Pigeons? Yes. Each aircraft carried two pigeons – on operational sorties anyway – and these would be taken into the dinghy, if ditching became necessary and used to send messages back to base giving map references for rescue purposes.

I well remember a poster which seemed to appear on many station notice boards during the war. Against a background of searchlights, it showed two pigeons flying side by side each having only a scant number of feathers. One is wide eyed and portrayed as saying to the other, 'My dear the flak was awful'! Seen in its war context it seemed humorous at the time but, alas, it has lost its impact over the years.

Apart from flying, a fair amount of time was allocated to safety matters such as parachute training and ditching drill.* One very important training aspect involved flying at heights over 10,000 feet. Each crew position had a supply of oxygen, but when it became necessary to move from one place to another, a portable oxygen bottle had to be used.† No problem? Yes, of course, but there was a tendency for crew members to take chances on an I'll-be-OK-for-a-short-while basis and this had resulted in fatalities. To prove the danger of the lack of oxygen, the whole crew were seated in a decompression chamber and taken up to the equivalent altitude of 15,000 feet. None felt any different at this height as you might expect. After return to normal ground level pressure, we all left the chamber except for the skipper. He remained and we gathered around the window outside to observe his second trip to high altitude but, this time, he was given some easy sums to do at regular intervals. The effect was quite astonishing. At 11,000 feet he was capable of accepting instructions, but at a marginally slower rate. However, his calculations were accurate. At 15,000 feet he was definitely slowing down, his writing became untidy and his sums inaccurate. At 20,000 feet he

* Training in launching and entering a dinghy after forced landing in the sea.
† A visit to the Elsan toilet at the rear of the plane, for example.

45

was almost incapable of accepting instructions or dealing with the maths, and instead, gazed around vacantly. The reverse, of course, happened when the air pressure was increased and he returned to normal again. After leaving the chamber he said he was convinced that he was fully in control of his faculties all the time, because he felt confidently normal throughout the test. However, the evidence of his working sheet was indisputable and the point had been well made. Lack of oxygen has exactly the same effect as drinking alcohol, and I have often thought since, when great publicity is given to drink/drive problems, that use could be made of this equipment to demonstrate to the public the dangers of misusing alcohol. It might convince those people who claim that they drive better after a few drinks that they are wrong. There is no doubt that driver's reactions and judgements do, in fact, start to deteriorate as soon as alcohol enters the bloodstream. This may sound like the writing of a bigoted total abstainer. I'm not – but I don't drink and drive.

About this time Chic wrote to me with good news. Some old friends of the family living in nearby Doncaster had asked her if she would like to stay with them for the balance of my time at Lindholme and she accepted the invitation. This unexpected offer had been too good to miss and in due course I hied myself to Doncaster Railway Station to await the arrival of my wife and little daughter. The train drew up to the platform and Chic appeared holding Valerie in her arms. She gently lowered Bowie (her nickname based on her own pronunciation) to the ground and, to my delight, let her toddle towards me with arms outstretched. She had been walking for a week but Chic had kept the news as a surprise ... I picked her up equally astonished that she knew me, since our meetings had been few and far between. She had, of course, been primed about meeting Daddy and knew that I existed through saying goodnight to my photograph each evening. However the surprise demonstration Chic had laid on had worked perfectly and not misfired by Bowie turning away with fear or hiding, shyly, behind her mother's skirt ... This incident brought home to me the enormity of my present situation. What had I done? Here I was on the brink of taking part in a hazardous operational tour. Was it right for one to have volunteered to do so as a family man – should my duty to my wife and young daughter have taken precedence over patriotic duty? I could not answer this but the questions posed gave much scope for critical examination of one's motives. Why had I volunteered? Was it because of boyish foolishness or bravado: the need to boost one's ego or seek quick promotion; the challenge of adventure, a compelling retributive ambition or power motive? I could not reach any conclusion then, nor have I been able to subsequently. Sometimes, I ponder on what it is in man which drives him to take part in the ultimate of his profession, such as climbing Everest, sailing a yacht around the world alone, or driving a racing car around Brands Hatch at enormous speeds. I suggest it may be due to an inborn urge or perhaps this is only part of the answer to a complex question. Possibly the whole is a mixture of some of the factors mentioned above and perhaps a few more. Who knows?

Our stay in Doncaster with Doris and Arnold Pygott was a much appreciated and pleasant interlude, and Chic and I were eternally grateful to them for their kindness during those precious and uncertain days. I had known Doris since childhood when her family owned a country cottage at Cleatlam, near Barnard Castle. My family use to spend holidays in a house nearby and I used to play cricket with her brothers morning and afternoon, day after day, during those long warm summers of the late 20s and early 30s. We reminisced at length about those far-off, happy, carefree days.

As a crew, our time at Lindholme had run its course and we were adjudged now to be fully trained to deal with whatever would be required. Soon we would be posted to an operational squadron. At this time I had only flown 30 hours by day and 5 hours by night. The latter figure seemed to be woefully small in view of the fact that most of our future flying would be at night yet, in the event, it sufficed.

Chapter 7

The Curtain Rises

The time had arrived for us to take part in raids over enemy territory. It was the end of a long period of training for the crew generally and all that we had learnt would now be put to good use by those who directed Bomber Command under the very capable leadership of its commander-in-chief, Air Chief Marshal Sir Arthur Harris – usually referred to as 'Butch' by squadron personnel.

It was late February 1943 when we arrived at our operational unit. This was No 12 Squadron based at RAF Wickenby, one of the many temporary airfields which sprang up in the eastern half of England during the war. It was situated about 10 miles east of Lincoln and was a compactly built unit, more so than many other stations I knew, which seemingly spread themselves haphazardly over the landscape. The main gate, with its inevitable guard room, was close by the administration centre and maintenance buildings – the control tower was also near at hand. The billets, messes and briefing room etc were all situated on a road behind the administrative block. It was on this road that we would live for the next few months – in a Nissen hut. It wasn't a palace but it had space and was big enough to house six of us comfortably. It was quite warm even in early spring time. Trevor being the only commissioned member of the crew was housed elsewhere in greater comfort as appropriate to an officer and a gentleman.

Wickenby was a satellite station of RAF Binbrook and was commanded by Wing Commander Woods – Winco or sometimes Timber for short. At that time 12 Squadron was the only squadron on the station, although it had more than the normal complement of aircraft because a third flight had been added from which it was hoped to form a new 626 Squadron in due course but more about that later.

'Shiny' 12, as it was known, was a squadron with great tradition dating back to the First World War. Its insignia bore the head of a fox and its motto 'Leads the Field' dates back to the time when the squadron was equipped with Fairy Fox aircraft. They were painted silver, with metal cowlings which gave rise to the name. It was therefore quite appropriate... Two of its members had already received VCs in 1940.

With all the training over how did we feel? What would the future hold? Perhaps we felt the way a chairman described his company's performance by saying 'it is hard to believe that last year we were teetering on the brink of a precipice, but this year we are set to take a flying leap forward'.

After a few local trips, we didn't have long to wait until we were summoned to the briefing room. Our emotions would now be put to the test.

Briefing was an essential prelude to any sortie... A special large room was set aside for this purpose. It accommodated about 30 crews sitting in rows facing the platform which was occupied by those responsible for briefing, including the station commander, section leaders (navigation, gunnery etc), meteorological and intelligence officers. The briefing itself was informative and full of interest. Attention was always centred on a huge map of the relevant portion of Europe on which the more heavily defended parts of Germany and the target for the night were shown. Information about the route to and from the target and its importance to the enemy's war effort was given, along with details of the number of aircraft taking part, the weight and type of bombs to be carried, the type of pathfinder target indicator flares to be used,* the weather to be expected with

---

* Flares were carried by the Pathfinder Force – PFF for short – to indicate the area to be bombed. Coloured flares would burst at about 500 feet and cascade to the ground and remain burning for some minutes. A red target indicator – sometimes referred to as a ground marker – was usually regarded as the more accurate and appeared every 10 minutes backed up, between times, by green flares.

comments on cloud amounts, fog amounts or thunderstorm risk, special tactics for the night and any other intelligence matter, such as diversionary raids.

Although briefing was a subject which had such serious implications for all involved, paradoxically, it often led to humorous asides by the speaker which engendered spontaneous repartee between the floor and the platform. In some way this generated a feeling of togetherness and even if the target was distant or heavily defended it created a sense of collective security.

It was early March 1943 when we began actively operating, just in time for the Battle of the Ruhr which we (along with other targets) would visit seventeen times during the coming weeks. We did in fact take off for Nuremburg on 8 March 1943 but for the first and only time during our tour, one of the upper hatches blew off and other faults developed. We therefore had to abandon the operation and after dumping our bombs in the North Sea, return to base. What a very undistinguished start to our tour and what an anticlimax, having been all keyed-up and then to limp home with nothing to show for our endeavours. However, we were to have another attempt to complete our first 'op' on the following night.

We sat in the briefing room in neat rows waiting for all to be revealed. Everyone was in place on the platform with the exception of the station commander. Shortly the buzz of conversation ceased as he appeared and we all stood up. We were motioned to sit and all eyes were turned to the map board which, of course, was covered. After a few words by Winco Woods the nod was given and the curtain started to rise. The route line, in dog-leg fashion, plunged deep into the south-east of Germany to Munich. It looked, and in fact was, a long way over enemy territory and therefore appeared to be a difficult target for an inexperienced crew to attempt. However, in our favour was the fact that Maurice, our skipper, had flown two operations with an experienced crew as second pilot and had therefore seen, at first hand, at least something of what to expect. Further, the indirect route to and from the target took us round, rather than through the more heavily defended areas.

Our bomb load comprised 1 × 4,000lb bomb – usually known as a 'cookie' – 540 × 4lb and 24 × 30lb incendiary bombs. We became very used to carrying this combination of bombs with variations to

F/Lt Lancaster (aptly named) setting astride a 'cookie' (4,000lb bomb). The trolly at rear contains canisters of incendiary bombs

the incendiary load according to the distance of the target. The raid was relatively small with less than 300 aircraft. No problems were encountered on the way out and we were interested in seeing the work of the Pathfinder Squadrons for the first time. We were impressed, dead on time the target indicators cascaded down... Greens grouping around the red. Not exactly in orderly fashion, of course, rather more ragged with irregular gaps. But, the markers were quite clear and these along with a sea of white incendiary bombs, intermittent HE bomb explosions and developing fires, combined with the blue-white shafts of the searchlights to make a very colourful and pretty, if dangerous, scene. Visibility was clear and Tommy experienced no difficulty in selecting the best spot in the centre of the group of target indicators. He seemed confident with the result, as well he might, since the raid was a success. Three thousand buildings were damaged or destroyed, along with the BMW Works aero-engine shops which were put out of action for six weeks. Although flak had been heavy over the target area, no fighters were seen and no difficulty was experienced from interception on the way home.

This had been a long trip of some eight hours and we arrived back at base after 4 a.m. There was much to do after landing. It was necessary to shed our flying clothing and kit in the locker room and return the parachutes to the store for care and maintenance. We then had to proceed to the debriefing room where the entire crew, armed with mugs of tea or coffee, huddled round the intelligence officer and in turn gave an account of any incident of note. Debriefing was not taken lightly. It was a serious attempt to extract and record as much worthwhile information as possible on the bombing offensive, while events were still fresh in the mind. As a matter of interest it is this process which was responsible, in the main, for the vast quantity of well documented information on Bomber Command's activities, which is currently freely available at the Public Record Office at Kew. After debriefing, a visit to the mess for that highlight of any operation – the egg and bacon breakfast – then off to bed. But the grey light of dawn had already broken before we were able to turn back the sheets.

When I visited Munich some twenty years later on holiday, I found it hard to believe that anyone should wish to attack this beautiful city so savagely, situated as it is, in the shadow of the peaceful and attractive Tyrolean Hills . . . but *c'est la guerre.*

We wondered if the experience we had gained from the Munich raid would form a pattern for things to come. We somehow doubted if it would be so, but the question was still in our minds, when the next day we were called to the briefing room again. This time it was Stuttgart and we would take a 'cookie' and 690 × 4lb and 32 × 30lb incendiary bombs. This important industrial centre in south-west Germany was somewhat nearer than Munich, evidenced by the total flying time which was shorter by one hour and twenty minutes. Even so, it was still a fairly lengthy flight but again the route dodged the really heavily defended areas.

Rather more than 300 aircraft would take part and no problems were encountered on the outward run. Conditions were generally good with no cloud and only thin haze over the target. With PFF markers clearly showing, a repetition of the performance two nights previously seemed possible. But it was not to be so. Something had gone wrong. Either the PFF markers were inaccurate or the Germans had laid dummy flares. Whichever the case, many of the 300 bombers had wasted their efforts and damage to Stuttgart was confined to residential property. Fortunately, losses to Bomber Command were below average.

Well, at least we did tumble into bed a little earlier, which was to our benefit, because we were surprised later in the day to be called to operate again. Three trips in four days, when the previous two had virtually involved all-night sessions seemed a little excessive. Under training there had been times when we felt very much under pressure, but it was relatively nothing compared with the topsy-turvy turmoil of night activity from dusk to dawn we were now experiencing. No doubt the operations staff had problems with weather factors/flying conditions when planning raids, but Butch Harris would decide and we would unquestioningly carry out his commands.

It was inevitable that sooner or later a target in the 'Happy Valley' – our customary name for the Ruhr – would be chosen and sure enough, possibly the most familiar name in that area was nominated – ESSEN. To me the name of this place had a cold metallic chink about it, probably due to the fact that it was the well-known home of Krupps and the very centre of the German arms industry. Consequently, it had been attacked many times since 1940. Not that it had been damaged to any extent. There were problems... In common with other Ruhr towns, industrial haze and smoke screens often obscured targets making life difficult for bomb aimers. However, since the inception of the Pathfinder Force in late 1942 and with better navigational aids, target finding and target marking equipment introduced in early 1943, there was a chance that we might do a little better.

Our load was composed of the usual cookie and mixed incendiary bombs but, this time 450 aircraft would take part... Unlike other raids, we were given a rendezvous time over the north Norfolk coast. A single vertical searchlight would be switched on at Sheringham at dusk and this we would circle until the moment came to set course for the Ruhr. Interesting stuff this, or so we thought, and after take-off we made our way towards the appointed location. Ahead the searchlight probed the darkening sky. We expected to see many other

THE CURTAIN RISES

aircraft and it was obviously prudent to keep a sharp look-out but, we were quite unprepared for what was about to happen. As we neared the searchlight, in half light, we found a swarm of bombers swirling around like bees above a disturbed apiary... Lancasters to the left, right, above and below and some even crossing and flying against the main stream... Strewth... I was in a sweat and with eyes like saucers and wildly rotating my turret, I managed to keep some sort of terse commentary going. Those of us who had seen what was going on (Maurice, Harry, Tommy and self) were more than glad when the time came to set course. It was standard practice for this rendezvous point to be used for raids to the east and no doubt there was a good reason for this. However, we decided as a crew that, in future, we would not go anywhere near the searchlight but would stand off elsewhere instead. I did not see or hear of any collisions taking place at Sheringham, but it seemed inevitable that such would occur sooner or later.

Climbing over the North Sea to operational height it was not long until we reached the Dutch coast to the accompaniment of sporadic flak and after 20 minutes, or so, we could see in the distance that the Ruhr was getting very excited about our visit. Heavy flak was being pumped up at an enormous rate. As far as we were concerned it was to no avail, we sailed in and, despite the ground haze Tommy could easily see the Pathfinder's ground marker and bombed accordingly. We then set course for home. On this occasion, Ken Swann (see photograph page 92), who was flying some way ahead of us, reported that bomb bursts were seen on the edge of the markers and large fires were concentrated. He was right and very observant... the raid had been a success due mainly to OBOE marking by PFF Mosquito aircraft. Krupps factory had become the centre of bombing and had suffered more damage than on any other raid.

To explain OBOE I cannot do better than quote Martin Middlebrook:* 'OBOE was a blind bombing device fitted to an aircraft controlled from ground stations in England. Two stations transmitted pulses which were picked up by the (Pathfinder) aircraft and retransmitted to the ground stations again. The aircraft receiving the OBOE signals, used the pulses to keep itself on the correct track in order

---
* *The Bomber Command War Diaries*, Martin Middlebrook and Chris Everitt.

to pass over the target; the stations in England by measuring the time taken to receive the pulses back again calculated the aircraft's exact position and sent a short signal at the moment when the marker bombs should be released. An average bomb aiming error of less than 300 yards could be achieved. Mosquito aircraft which could fly up to 30,000 feet and faster than any bomber were used on the Ruhr raids particularly, but could not be used on targets deeper into Germany, due to the effects of the earth's curvature.'

Following Essen, we were left alone until the end of the month when Duisburg was nominated as the target. In company with 450 aircraft we set out with the usual bomb load for delivery to this sizeable Ruhr town concerned with coal, iron and other industries. However, we were prevented from bombing accurately by cloud over the target. Most reports by crew captains spoke of 10/10ths cloud and added that glow on cloud cover suggested scattered fires. This was about the strength of the raid. In fact, due to pathfinding difficulties the Mosquitoes had not been able to operate properly and could not repeat their previous success. A pity, but in consequence the raid had to be written off as a failure.

Chapter 8

The Big One

An immediate and electrifying buzz of mixed comments filled the air of the briefing room some three nights later. The curtain rose to reveal a red ribbon stretching eastwards across the map to Berlin... Wow... and 400 aircraft would take part... I dare say that most of us, experienced or otherwise, felt a little apprehensive at the prospect of such a distant raid penetrating deeply into German territory, but this was quickly set to one side since the target was of supreme importance. Without doubt, one felt that the war with all its horrors was forcibly being brought home to the German population despite earlier predictions of Herman Goering, the Luftwaffe Chief, that no bomber would penetrate their defences. To take part in laying a bomb on the very doorstep of Hitler's Third Reich was as much as any bomber crew could ask for and, in my case, was some retribution for the narrow squeaks I experienced in air raids on Birmingham, and for the suffering the German bombers had caused at home earlier in the Blitz of 1940–41. Additionally, I would never forget the horrific raid on Coventry which I watched all night from Hodgehill Common.

I certainly felt that this raid on Berlin was the ultimate purpose of all the training and effort made to date. This same sense of purpose was evident in the briefing room. Not that anyone underestimated the difficulties. Berlin was no easy target. Situated as it is, near the eastern border of Germany it would require about four hours' flying time over enemy-controlled territory. One could be sure that the Huns would do their utmost to defend their capital. It would be a needle match and we would have to be more than usually watchful. As it happened the outward flight, once through the heavily defended zone, was very quiet but nearer the target the intensity of the flak barrage was similar to that of the Ruhr.

On the approach to Berlin, which was already illuminated by flares, incendiary bombs, fires and searchlights, I could clearly see that we had arrived in company with many other Lancasters – surely a tribute to the navigators for their skill and timing. We had not experienced this type of concentration before but, from my mid-upper turret, I was well placed to watch for the possibility of being bombed from those flying higher . . . Suddenly two hundred feet above I saw a Lanc was closing in, I yelped a warning to Maurice and he spotted it – just in time we edged over to port a little. In the rosy glow from the ground, the threatening spectacle of a big cookie and rows of incendiary containers in the bomb bay of the aircraft flying overhead was not a pretty sight. This called for cool judgement from Maurice, since to put Tommy, our bomb aimer, off his run and circle round again for another bombing attempt would not have been popular. It would have increased the time over the target area and, more importantly, would inevitably mean flying against the incoming bomber stream which could prove disastrous. Anyhow, we managed to avoid being bombed from above and our bombs missed those below . . . Just after this an Fw 190 whipped in head on but instead of attacking us, dived underneath, then slightly to port.* Within seconds another Lancaster appeared from below with flames streaming from the length of the trailing edge of its wings. Slowly it turned away, nose down, gathering momentum and developing tail-spin, as it fell. I watched for as long as I dared but, as far as I could see, no one escaped . . .

There was a slight ground haze but the PFF markers were clear and Tommy had bombed these. So far as we and the other crews from Shiny 12 were concerned, Berlin was well and truly bombed that night, even if the centre had been missed. Many raging fires

---

* I judged that he was slightly off the line required to shoot at us. The pilot probably saw a better target below and made for it. Combat actions in the air or near misses are very quick, split-second affairs and I was not able to bring my guns to bear on him. Obviously our luck was another's misfortune.

were seen and, fortunately, Bomber Command's casualties were extraordinarily low.

After the bombing run it was discovered that we had a bomb hang-up, but with a quick dive and climb Maurice was able to shake it free and we set course for home. Again, the same almost eerie quietness descended on us and, apart from the occasional shudder of the airframe when crossing someone's slipstream, we had an unmolested journey back. We had only coastal defences to contend with before flying silently, nose down, over the North Sea and back to base.

As the losses that night were much lighter than usual, it would appear that the Huns had been taken by surprise and had concentrated their efforts elsewhere. Someone's head would surely roll!

So, we now had five raids to our credit including the 'big one' but we still had a lot to learn and there was no room for cockiness, or relaxation of the discipline we had subconsciously imposed on ourselves. As a crew we were working well together which was all to the good and, for my part, I had a lot of confidence in the other crew members.

On most raids to date we had been aware of large explosions in the sky from time to time. These occurred usually at a height of between 19,000 and 20,000 feet. Seemingly, they appeared anywhere without warning, or for any tangible reason... In spectacular fashion, a huge central fire ball emitted streams of white and coloured lights which slowly cascaded downwards behind a spirally burning nucleus. All crews were used to seeing these (apparently) pyrotechnical displays, which were known as 'Scarecrows'. Their existence was openly discussed by aircrew generally and sometimes mentioned at briefing sessions but, the question which no one could answer was 'what were these phenomena'? Because there was no definite information available, it was generally assumed that the Germans had projectiles of some sort which could simulate the explosion and disintegration of bomber aircraft in the hope that these could lead, ultimately, to the lowering of morale amongst aircrew.

One would expect that a large explosion whether of a missile or an exploding aircraft would initiate a shock wave, which would be felt by any aircraft flying within the vicinity, but in my experience this never occurred and I find it hard to give any logical reason... For certain, some of the explosions (perhaps all) must have come from actual bombers being blown to pieces. No two incidents of this type would appear exactly alike or follow the same pattern. Much, I suppose, would depend on the quantity of fuel aboard, the type of bomb load, type of pyrotechnics (eg flares) carried and which part of the aircraft was hit etc. It may be, therefore, that inconsistencies in accounts reported by aircrew led to the conclusion that, at least, some of the explosions were, somehow or other, created by the enemy for the reason given above. During the war no one could be certain about Scarecrows and therefore the possibility of their existence could never be denied by our intelligence officers. I don't blame them – they had no way of knowing at that time. In a strange way this was an advantage since, as far as we were concerned, any large explosion in the dark sky was adjudged to be a Scarecrow and therefore had no effect on our morale.

After the war, inquiries were made in Germany about Scarecrows. Those who served on anti-aircraft gun sites and commanded posts were closely questioned, but none would admit having intentionally fired a projectile which could simulate an exploding aircraft. Apart from this, militarily it would not make sense just to try and scare bomber crews. The aim of firing missiles at the bomber stream must inevitably have been to damage or destroy them, if possible. There would be no point in providing a free Guy Fawkes-night display. However, it may well be that some witnesses are not fully convinced by the Germans' denials and therefore in these circumstances perhaps the phenomena of Scarecrows will remain one of the minor mysteries of the Second World War.

SUMMARY FOR MARCH 1943

Date	Take-off time	Aircraft	Pilot	Duty	Flying time
9	20.00	Lancaster W	Sgt. Wells	Operations	MUNICH 8.00 hrs
11	20.00	" Z	"	"	STUTTGART 6.40 "
12	19.40	" Z	"	"	ESSEN 4.25 "
24	20.00	" W	"	"	DUISBERG 3.55 "
27	20.25	" W	"	"	BERLIN 6.40 "

What would the next month bring? It turned out to be a mixed bag again but the variety was as full of interest as it was wide ranging.

Chapter 9

Fear Is an Ally

We all experience fear to some degree. It is just as well since an individual totally without fear – if such exists – would be a menace to himself and those around him.

Fear of flying and particularly operational flying, provided that it is controlled, is as good a safety factor as any. It imposes a discipline, which obliges one to adhere pedantically to the rules, to make sure that equipment is fully serviceable and that personal fitness, both mental and physical, is as high as possible. In other words, fear of the consequences promotes a dedication to the job in hand and this can help, paradoxically, to overcome one's apprehensions. In other words, it concentrates the mind. During my tour with 12 Squadron, I suppose, I inadvertently observed my colleagues in their attitude and I was never aware that any of them were openly afraid. I can say with impunity that there was no outward signs of stress. For example, there were no heated arguments or emotional outbursts. No crew member crept into a corner and silently brooded or sought to drown his sorrows in excessive alcohol. These were all good indications of calm and healthy mental dispositions. High spirits, of course, abounded as one would expect amongst a collection of chaps the majority of whom were in their early twenties. One time fear could have surfaced was at briefing prior to a raid and waiting time before take off, but none was discernible – due, I suggest, to the fact that generally we were too busy with our preparations.

The worst charge that the authorities could level at aircrew personnel was known as LMF – Lack of Moral Fibre – refusal to fly operationally was looked upon by those in command as something approaching desertion in the face of the enemy and it had the most serious consequences. I did not witness any LMF cases at first hand, though I believe one occurred at Wickenby in the following year. I have no idea what his problem was. It could have been fear or perhaps for religious reasons or other conscience grounds. Whatever – the penalty was loss of rank in full view of all personnel followed by a posting elsewhere or discharge (if commissioned) and recall with demotion to the other ranks. It could be said perhaps that some aircrew members were more afraid of being labelled LMF than they were of sticking out their necks but I doubt this. Most were optimists and, as with car crashes, disasters were things that always happened to other chaps. Nevertheless, all operational aircrew were aware that losses averaged about five per cent per raid. No official figures were available at the time but subsequently it was divulged that during the war, 12 Squadron had the highest percentage losses in Group 1 and the second highest in Bomber Command. Therefore, anyone operating was due for the 'chop' by the time 20 operations were completed and the odds of finishing a tour of 30 operations were much against. This situation would often be shrugged off in a detached manner when perhaps on inquiring from an acquaintance 'dicing tonight'? – the cheerful reply with a grin could be 'Yes, Junk-Junk, chop-chop' – a slang reference to the possibility of being shot down by a Junkers 88 night-fighter. If you cannot accept that individuals could become so detached from actuality, let me say that the day-to-day setting was unreal. Although the RAF station with its bombers, bombs, guns, ammunition and similar objects, evidenced its warlike nature, everything else away from the airfield remained superficially calm and divorced from the reality of its horrifying destructive potential. When not on ops or preparing, much of the time one could therefore relax and lead a normal carefree service life. Believe it or not, in our hut we rarely spoke of flying or ops unless something funny had happened. It seemed, in a way, to be similar to coming home from the office or work and changing into something more comfortable and settling down to lead one's other life. In other words, war was war and away from it life was life.

The Germans did their best to deter aircrews with their night-fighters, light and heavy flak barrages. Night-fighters were a constant threat. They could attack at any time on the way to, over, or on the way back from, a target. Even over base and on landing the threat was always present. Heavy flak barrages were a different matter. Seen from the distance, especially when approaching the Ruhr, they seemed to form a solid impenetrable barrier. The sky between 18,000 and 20,000 feet appeared to be filled with the flashing of exploding shells scintillating in the thin clear air but the barrier effect was an illusion due to foreshortening. Once entered, it became obvious that the flak wall was not solid, but spread over a considerable distance in depth. Thus, apart from an occasional wump and bucking of the aircraft (sometimes as bad as driving an 'old banger' over a bumpy road) along with accompanying puffs of black smoke, the reality was less scaring than one might imagine. Certainly, some aircraft did receive direct hits and suffered severe or terminal damage, but the risk of this happening was not high. One became very used to the situation and, since most aircraft received only superficial damage from shrapnel, in my experience, the majority of aircrew regarded heavy flak barrages as more of a nuisance than a hazard.

Apart from night-fighters, searchlights were a real menace – not in themselves, of course, but because of the dangers which would inevitably follow. Lurking silently and insidiously in the background, searchlights were very efficient and the threat of being singled out for special treatment was always present. We were 'coned' by searchlights three times at Bochum, Stettin and Aachen. On each occasion, without warning we were picked out by a radar-controlled master searchlight, followed almost immediately by a ring of perhaps thirty satellites. Once caught, there was no alternative but to take whatever attack was coming. However, to say the least, it certainly was not pleasant but one was preoccupied with the possibility of fighter attack; the difficulty of avoiding being blinded temporarily by searchlights thus losing night vision and the heavy concentration of anti-aircraft fire. The writhing and jinking of the aircraft caused by the skipper trying to escape from the beams, was quite an experience. It was similar to riding involuntarily on a huge long roller-coaster trip – with which Blackpool could not compete – and, for added interest, being pelted with stones intermittently. The difference was that there was no charge – it was all for free, by courtesy of the Hun.

Some people obviously are more afraid than others of life's hazards. Much I suppose depends on the make-up of the individual and his or her reaction to circumstances. I have experienced fear on the M1 Motorway when overtaking huge container lorries at 70 mph in torrential rain and spray-obliterated vision for a few seconds, or when suddenly running into a blanket of fog at night. I have been afraid when an unexpected gust of wind threatened to blow me from the top of a ladder, or before seeing the dentist. I therefore regard myself as average in this respect... Why then was I not afraid when flying operationally? Well, as I have tried to show here it is nullified by preoccupation with the job in hand. After much soul searching, I am convinced that a hundred per cent concentration prevented those niggling doubts and fears from taking over. In this analysis of my reaction to fear and, indeed possibly that of my crew, I am reminded of the words of Coleridge – 'what begins in fear usually ends in folly'. I see his point if fear is allowed to take over, but I would rather say that 'fear is an ally... a safety device... but to panic is folly'.

The antonym of fear is morale. If one takes the latter to mean confidence and discipline, pride, fixity of purpose and faith in the cause fought for – then fear cannot win the day. Good morale in the RAF was evinced in a saying oft heard – 'press on regardless'. There were very many good examples of this in Bomber Command during the war. There had to be... wars are not won without it. Those who criticise the Second World War efforts of operational squadrons – British or American – today, simply have no idea of what war was about. Let me give you an example.

The day before our last raid on Duisburg we, as a crew, were standing by our Lancaster prior to take off for a night-flying test. The skipper of the kite in the adjacent bay sauntered over to us and, as he approached, we could see that he was in a frightful mess. He had two black eyes and multiple lacerations to his face. 'How had that happened, Alec'? was the obvious question. This amiable diminutive Aussie pilot, who would have looked more at home flying Spitfires than handling Lancaster bombers, explained that he had been sitting in the cockpit the previous day when the locks were being taken off the controls. It happened to be a very windy day and he had literally wrapped himself around the joy-stick to keep it steady, when a sudden squall had forcefully thrust the control forward and catapulted him via the instrument panel onto the windscreen. The result was horrific. He should, of course, have reported sick and had he done so he would probably have rested from flying duties for a few days at least. But no, he pressed on regardless and took his crew on to the Duisburg raid. Alas, they failed to return. Fate had dealt a severe blow. We were very sorry.

Chapter 10

Germany 4 Italy 2

Earlier I described Maurice, our skipper, as a quiet and unassuming chap. He was the epitome of a good living, helpful and neighbourly type but give him an aeroplane and his saintly character changed to devilry. His passion was low flying – the lower the better... During the early part of April we had a short break from operational duties due to unsuitable weather conditions. Our first trip was in daylight when, much to Maurice's delight, we were dispatched on a low formation flying exercise. It was repeated four days later and we wondered, vaguely, what significance, if any, could be attached to these outings. Each sortie lasted for over an hour, and were much enjoyed as a romp, even if they were not appreciated by the local farmers and the rural population.

Between these two events we were twice called upon to devote our attention to the Fatherland... Groans rose from the floor as the first target was to be Essen again. This location, important as it was, had understandably, received much attention since 1940 and had been one of the targets visited by an earlier 1,000 bomber raid, when experiments in saturating the enemy's defences, by sheer weight of numbers, were being conducted.

On this occasion about 350 aircraft would take part, each carrying the usual mixture of high explosive and incendiary bombs. There was no cloud over the target, which was fortunate since the weather forecasters had been uncertain as to the conditions we could expect.

In the event, Tommy could clearly see the target markers and did his bombing. We turned for home satisfied that we had witnessed another successful raid. However, it proved to be not quite as effective as the previous raid on Essen, in which Krupps had been severely damaged. Nevertheless, widespread damage had been sustained by certain areas of the target area but, unfortunately Bomber Command losses were above average with 22 aircraft missing. This amounted to six per cent of the raiding force.

> Second lesson for Essen
> But we'll keep 'em guessin'
> Next day will reveal
> We'll push off to Kiel
> And make an almighty mess in!

So, the next trip was to the big naval port of Kiel. This was to be a larger raid with something nearer 600 aircraft taking part. It was known that cloudy conditions would prevail but, since German naval vessels were expected to be in or near the port, the opportunity could not be missed. Accordingly, the bomb load carried by the Lancasters changed. This time, according to the group (our group) report Lancasters would each carry 11 × 1,000 general purpose bombs, but my memory is that armour piercing bombs were used on this occasion.* Wellingtons within the Group however, would generally carry only incendiary bombs except for those which had been converted to carry a cookie.

After a surprisingly long sea leg, we noticed that the islands off the Dutch coast, including Texel, were heavily defended. They bristled with guns and had to be respected. Just after crossing the coast on the outward leg 10/10ths cloud developed, as forecast, at 10,000 feet.

Occasionally white parachute flares would illuminate the scene. It was not obvious whether these had been dropped by PFF as track indicators, or if enemy fighter aircraft were responsible for them. Perhaps it was a combination of both but, whatever the case, because

---

* Bomber Command was split into five operational groups – 1 to 5, a sixth was added later. The Pathfinder Group was number 8. A sample portion of a Group 1 Summary appears as in the appendices.

GERMANY 4 ITALY 2

A constructed photograph of the cien prior to take-off for a raid on Kiel.
L to R- Ray, Trevor, Joe, Tommy, Harry and Doug

of the cloud cover some 10,000 feet below, a good proportion of the bomber force could be seen silhouetted against a white sheet, as it were. It was quite an inspiring sight to look down and see this apparently slow-moving river of Halifax, Stirling and Wellington bombers (which generally flew at lower heights than Lancasters) wending their way five abreast in a staggered procession, as far as the eye could see. What a demonstration of power! Only once during the tour were we to witness anything like it. Had it been shown on a cinema screen, I could imagine that it would have had a fanfare, or a stirring musical accompaniment from Elgar's Pomp and Circumstance March – or both.

Although we could see the horde of bombers below, I reflected that they would not generally be aware of each other ... In the same way any night-fighter flying, say, 5,000 feet above would be able to see the whole of the Lancaster force (two hundred plus) but, so far as I was concerned, apart from occasional sightings of bombers nearby, the strength of the surrounding force was not evident. It was, however, disconcerting to realise the vulnerable position of the bomber force. With the advantage of height, fighters would have been able to pick at random. But where were they? In fact losses for the night were well below average, so obviously there must have been some intervenient factor but just what, one could only guess.

The outcome of the raid was not good. Most crews reported heavy cloud cover and were unable to judge whether they had found the target. The weather had won the day – again. Perhaps the adverse conditions, which hindered Bomber Command, also hindered the night-fighters – who knows?

Between operational trips there was little to do in the area surrounding Wickenby, which was remotely situated in the flat Lincolnshire countryside. Even the local, the White Hart at Lissington, was not easily accessible. Lincoln itself teemed with airmen and, because of various pranks perpetrated by a few irresponsible bods, we were collectively regarded as *personae non gratae*. The Saracen's Head was the centre of social activity and known better as the crew room. It was said that occasionally the target for the night was an open secret here, and this led sometimes to bomb targets and bomb/fuel loads having to be changed at short notice. Whatever the truth in the former assertion I know not. Without doubt, bomb and fuel loads were changed on the day of a raid sometimes, but whether these were due to quick changes of target due to adverse weather conditions, or to tactical manoeuvres or for some other reason, one could only guess.

The lack of local entertainment facilities inevitably meant that leisure time was spent either in one's billet or in the mess playing table tennis or snooker. Stories of goings-on in both the officers' and sergeants' messes were rife – rugby games, debagging and footmarks over the ceiling were a few of the milder examples. Some stories, I am certain were true but others were probably apocryphal or, at least, grossly exaggerated... One incident I can vouch for occurred not at Wickenby but, I seem to remember, at Manby. One evening an Aussie pilot, determined to settle a bet, said that he would make an imprint of his bottom on the mess ceiling, which was a fair height. Tables were piled on top of one another to a point within 5 or 6 feet of the ceiling and then a wooden armchair was placed in position on top. The Aussie who had had his bare bottom liberally plastered with boot polish then climbed to the top of this somewhat rickety structure, grasped each arm of the chair and slowly rotated his body, in a controlled somersault movement, until his bottom touched the ceiling. He then pressed upwards firmly and left a very creditable imprint of his cheeks in the desired position. He returned to the floor to the accompaniment of thunderous applause. He certainly was a cool and skilful acrobat. I know not who eventually paid to clear up the mess. Boot polish would be very difficult to remove from the ceiling and I imagine that the back of the Aussie's underpants would remain a permanently peculiar colour. A sort of dark reminder of a dirty deed.

The next two raids were noteworthy more for their difficulty than their success. Both were on Duisburg on successive nights. On the first, more than 300 aircraft – a mixture of Lancasters, Wellingtons, Halifaxes and Stirlings – set off for the Dutch coast but then encountered solid cloud with tops up to 22,000 feet. Positive identification of the target was impossible. No crew apparently bombed on Pathfinder flares and most released their cargo through cloud on ETA (estimated time of arrival). A very hit-and-miss situation. In a scattered raid such as this, obviously some bombs fell on to the intended spot (like a blind man lashing out in a crowded room – he is almost bound to catch someone between the eyes) and some damage did occur in Duisburg, but nothing like the scale it should have been. Altogether a disappointing experience for us and all those taking part.

The next night only a small force of bombers were detailed for action and again solid cloud was encountered. The outcome was only a little better than the previous night. On the whole it is better to regard these two raids as non-events in the overall offensive against Germany, though to the relatives of those who died on both sides, the result would be only too real. In this raid eight Lancasters out of the 100 plus which took off for Duisburg were reported missing.

The full-moon period was approaching and we expected to stand down for a short time, but it was not safe to assume anything in the RAF; life was not like that. We waited patiently in the briefing room for all to be revealed. The curtain was raised and, surprise, surprise, the red route ribbon on the map trailed southwards over France then turned over the Alps and across the Bay of Genoa to Spezia on the west coast of northern Italy. A cheer rose from everybody because Italian trips were looked upon as relatively easier than those to Germany... and so it proved. More than 200 aircraft would take part, nearly all Lancasters, and Italian warships were known to be in the port. The force included seven cruisers amongst them the *Gorizia*, *Bolzano* and *Taranto*, also a mixture of destroyers and torpedo boats. We would carry 5 × 1,000lb bombs and a much reduced load of 180 × 4lb and 16 × 30lb incendiary bombs and our instructions were to attack the ships if they could be seen. Spezia must be the best part of 1,000 miles by the route to be taken – a long way from home should mechanical trouble develop or damage be sustained over or near the target. Fortunately, the Eighth Army had been doing well in North Africa and newly released airfields there were operational. If necessary we could divert to them, which was a comforting thought.

The route over France was quiet and although we flew near Paris I could not pinpoint its position. The Germans had obviously imposed their blackout restrictions as thoroughly as they had done in their own country but, in addition, they made sure that the Parisians complied – not an easy task. Eventually, we turned south-east over southern France and headed towards the mountains. The snow-covered Alps by moonlight are a sight not to be forgotten and interest was supplied, presumably, by members of the Maquis who let their presence be known by flashing lights and lighting fires here and there in the mountains and valleys as we flew over them. However, in the middle of this magnificent scenery I was enjoying, suddenly, nearly the whole turret was coated with a layer of ice. I reported this to the skipper who, to my surprise, did not seem too perturbed. As the Bay of Genoa loomed up, I changed position forward to the astrodome and maintained observation from there during the more dangerous period over the target.* We were to bomb at 9,000 feet – a much lower level than normal – consequently much more ground detail could be seen despite the fact that a smoke screen was operating to the north of the town and was drifting across the aiming point in the north-west wind. The fleet could not be seen and there was no alternative other than to bomb the port installations and town which could be more readily identified. Tommy was satisfied with his bombing run and, with bombs gone, we set course for home. Many bomb bursts were seen around the point of aim where fires started and rapidly gained a firm hold. A number of large explosions were observed in the same area during the attack, followed by others which were seen some twenty minutes after leaving the target. It is believed that heavy damage had been sustained by the dock area in Spezia. I returned to my obscured turret for the 'safe' part of the journey home but returned to the astrodome for the exit from northern France.

On return, as luck would have it, Wickenby was fogbound and we were diverted to Finmere near Bicester. We landed, had breakfast in the local mess and by 9 a.m. the fog had cleared at base and we were able to go back. On entering the turret I saw that the ice had melted but the moisture outside instead of being clear was distinctly yellow in colour. You may have guessed it, certainly the grins of those in the cockpit told the story. Maurice, not wanting to go down to the Elsan toilet (situated at the rear of the plane) on a long trip of nine hours plus, had taken a bottle with him. When full, Harry had emptied it out of the side window and the slipstream had done the rest. It happened to be my 25th birthday and I couldn't help thinking that this was a strange and unwanted christening. Fortu-

---

* Astrodome – a transparent observation dome on top of the fuselage used normally by navigators when taking astroshots.

nately we ran into rain on the way back to base which saved an argument as to who was going to wash down the turret. Back at base, after we had returned to our hut, a degree of leg pulling about this incident occurred in which it was agreed that 'few have been urinated on at such a great height'. However, in my best authoritative voice, I added that 'as senior crew member by age I must request' . . . cheers and chortles . . . 'that in future, cockpit crew should consume their own produce and' . . . but I was not able to complete the sentence since I had disappeared under an upturned bed.

Four days later we took part in a repeat raid on Spezia. This time a smaller force took part – less than 200 – and the same bomb load was carried. The moon had risen and we proceeded over France in quiet conditions, so much so that I can't, in fact, recall seeing any searchlights or flak north of Genoa. As an aid to navigation the Pathfinders were supposed to drop landmark flares over Lac du Bourget (Aix-les-Bains). We saw the flares but no lake and could only assume that they had been dropped slightly out of position. The weather was clear, the moon was high and the snow-covered ridges of the Alps ahead promised another scenic treat. As we rose over the peaks other Lancasters appeared and we flew together for a while through superb mountain vistas before slowly diverging due possibly to small navigation adjustments to course. The visibility conditions were extraordinary, at least fifty miles, I would judge, and possibly twice that distance but I failed to identify Mont Blanc, although it must have been visible. Eventually, as we descended gradually to a bomb height of 8,000 feet over the Bay of Genoa, the shoreline stood out clearly, dividing the plush coppice landmass from the luminous serenely calm sea. The whole scene was one of peaceful tranquillity.

On approach to Spezia unco-ordinated searchlights began crazy merry-go-round movements and some Italian gunners were hosepiping light flak all over the sky quite ineffectively. It was easy to imagine the defending crews gesticulating and shouting excitedly at one another and generally running about in all directions like headless chickens. Their performance was the antipathy of the cool, efficient, ruthless approach of the Germans which we respected.

However, the smokescreen was better this time and made the bomb aimer's job more difficult. Nevertheless, with the aid of red ground markers Tommy dropped his bombs and off we went. The raid was perhaps not so effective as on the previous occasion but was judged to have been concentrated and generally successful.

On the way home we noticed a respectable and steady searchlight cone over Turin the likes of which they did not even attempt at Spezia. If this was one of our chaps someone was really off course. How this could happen in such perfect flying conditions is beyond comprehension but a more likely explanation is that the local searchlight unit were just having a quiet training session to themselves.

Our return journey was quiet and without incident. We had been routed to fly over central London on our way back home for morale purposes, though I am not sure that all Londoners would appreciate a force of heavy bombers thundering over at 2,000 feet so early in the morning. However, our presence had been picked up by the BBC and the announcer who, after greeting us, mentioned to the world that the boys of Bomber Command were returning from a raid. He then played the RAF March in our honour. Trevor had been quick enough to pick up the broadcast and relay it over the intercom (I think he must have had prior warning of the event) and we all felt rather elated by our welcome home. We felt also that we deserved the two ice-cream cones, which would be painted on the side of our kite to record the trips, which involved about 4,000 miles and nearly 20 hours' flying time.

I never did find out what Maurice did with his bottle this time but I would not be surprised, if it had been dropped over the target. He possessed that type of humour.

>
> We were two gunners called Ray and Doug –
> We occupied turrets that weren't very snug.
> One night we took fright,
> When we saw a light
> Of a decoy – and that can't be good.
>
> We searched the horizons both near and far.
> Had the kite upside down – and the skipper played war
> 'Cause there weren't any fighters,
> We'd played silly blighters.
> It was Venus the planet – or some other star!
> (Ha-ha-ha.)

Chapter 11

A Low Blow

After a two-day break we were called to the briefing room again. The hours of darkness were reducing and the moon's phase was fully at its peak and would shine all night. Surely it could not be Spezia again – we had only just made it last time during the available dark hours (dawn, in fact, was breaking as we were returning over the French coast) but, as ever, we were in for a colossal surprise. The uncovered map revealed a track ribbon leading up over the North Sea, turning over Denmark and across the length of the Baltic Sea to Stettin... The best was yet to come. Wing Commander Woods stood up, paused, gazed around the crews over his 'half eyes' and with an impish smile, announced that we were to fly low level both ways below radar detection height. Near pandemonium broke out... Crumbs! Flying at zero feet to a target 600 miles away... We were all excited except Joe who, I think, was trying to weigh up what navigational problems might ensue... Whatever, it was going to be quite a night. The weather was set fair, the night cloudless and moonlit, and this would be in our favour. The bombing run would be made after a climb to 10,000 feet near the target. The bomb load was a cookie and the usual mixture of incendiary bombs. About 340 aircraft would take part but only Group 1 Lancasters would be flying low level... Groups 3 and 5 had the option of flying at low level or at 12,000 feet.

It was still light when we set off... Maurice was in his element as we hedge-hopped over the countryside and we sped along just missing this or that obstruction in a way that only he could. One wondered, at times, whether he had had previous low-level flying experience in his native New Zealand, crop spraying for instance, so deft was his touch... from my mid-upper observation point with its excellent all-round view, particularly forward, I really did admire his skill. The Lincolnshire coastline loomed ahead and the seals – always in great numbers around The Wash – must have dived for cover as we sped over the North Sea skimming the waves in the brilliantly clear weather. It was a long stretch over the sea to Denmark and there was much time to contemplate the 'joys' of ditching if anything should go wrong... God, there wouldn't be much time to act if anything happened and most likely we would just disappear into a cloud of spray... A clean sweep one might say. Such thoughts had to be firmly put to the back of one's mind. Eventually, the coast of Denmark came into view – landfall had been made accurately and right on time and we sped inland admiring the moonlit scenery and seeing everything in great detail. There was no hint of mist, even in the valleys, as one might have expected. The conditions were quite extraordinary and just as the weather men had forecast. They must have been pleased with themselves, since even local weather forecasting could be very dodgy during the war when based, as it was, on incomplete information and even worse having to produce it for an area 600 miles away.

The Danish fields, woods and villages glided peacefully by. The placid rural scenery with its orderly farms and barns was seemingly as far divorced from war as could be imagined. One could easily be lulled into a false sense of security but not for long, since a little later we flew over an army barracks and could see clearly groups of soldiers firing their rifles at us in a vain attempt to stem the tide (although I gave them full marks for trying). At another point Ray and I were able to fire several long bursts at an army convoy, we hoped to better effect. We were flying too low for searchlights or light flak to be used against us and the possibility of fighter attack was out of the question. So, for once as gunners we felt the power of being on the offensive, instead of our usual defensive role, on the way to the target. However, before leaving Denmark two long white trails of incendiary bombs could be seen burning on the ground. This was ominous and the indications were that two Lancasters were in trouble – but this is another long story which was confirmed after the war.

The Baltic Sea leg was uneventful although it was amusing and interesting to see red Verey lights being fired as a warning (of us as intruders) to local aircraft, when we were flying near their bases. Eventually, the time arrived for us to cross the coast and ascend to 10,000 feet. We were still some distance from Stettin when activity started in the target area. Flak bursting upwards in plenty; target markers and bombs falling in matching quantity, with the result that fires had already started, when we arrived and the town was 'getting it thick and fast'. Tommy dropped his contribution, as far as he could tell spot on a green marker and, satisfied, gave the signal to return home. Perhaps we were a little complacent when suddenly 'plink' – on came a master searchlight, followed almost immediately by a ring of possibly 20 or 30 satellite units. We were held in a searchlight cone and flashes on the ground indicated we were in for a heavy barrage. The flak which came up was concentrated and soon the air was filled with puffs of black smoke to the extent that one could smell it (similar to cordite). Fortunately, the exploding shells were not near enough to cause serious damage but we were taking a fair peppering of shrapnel. A little later I suddenly became aware that the port wing had been holed by light flak and the force of the slipstream was tearing the jagged metal skin. At the same time poor old Tommy, who had been behind the nose panel when this was partly holed, was forcibly blown backwards against the bulkhead. Although cut about the face and bleeding he was otherwise undamaged. Harry cleaned him up and did his best to plug the hole in the aircraft's nose with a Mae West (!) to avoid heat loss. Luckily for all of us a 20mm shell which embedded itself in the back of the skipper's seat did not explode. The plane bucked about in reaction to the nearer explosions, but Maurice kept the nose down and by weaving and jinking managed to dodge most of the onslaught. After what seemed to be an age and having lost a lot of height, thankfully we ran out of the searchlights' range ... Simultaneously, three sets of conversations started on the intercom. Maurice was speaking to Ray about the danger of fighter attack (bombers were always in danger from night-fighters lurking just outside searchlight range); Joe was seeking information from Tommy in order to try to establish our exact position and Harry wanted information from me on the extent and position of the damaged wing... Bad intercom drill? Well, yes perhaps, but the remarkable point is that each of us received and understood the message as appropriate but also knew the gist of what the other conversations were about, which in my case meant that I could still maintain watch as required and talk to Harry at the same time. This, I think is a good example of how individuals can, and do, concentrate and remain cool in time of emergency and danger.

Apart from the holed wing, the aircraft had received a good deal of superficial damage but overall was judged to be airworthy. The metal skin had ceased tearing and although the damage was situated too near the port flap for comfort, it probably would not affect its operation and efficiency. The loss of height did not matter, since we had to return to ground level anyway. Our course was set westerly and we headed for home over the Baltic Sea. All was going well but, after a while we saw a large cargo vessel ahead. We could easily see the ship against its light sea background. On the other hand, we judged that it would be hard for them to see us against a low sky/land horizon and moving quickly. With this advantage we thought it safe to attack – not that eight .303 Browning peashooters would do all that much damage, but the patter of tiny bullets on their decks might make them hop about a bit. So, being in the advantageous position to judge when the rear gunner and bomb aimer in the front turret would be able to bring their guns to bear on the ship, it was left to me to say when. The word was duly given and we all fired, but, to our astonishment at the very same moment the ship's guns opened up with a blast of light flak, the effect of which was like flying down Oxford Street when the Christmas lights are switched on. A very pretty sight it was but not recommended to anyone wishing to live to a ripe old age. Subsequently, Maurice told me that his evasive action, when the ship opened up, was so violent that he nearly had a wing-tip in the water. He was warned just in time by an Aussie trainee who was acting as second pilot. Lady Luck was with us that night. A little later we saw another ship. But we dodged this one... We did not report our gunnery exchange at debriefing, though I feel we should have done so as a warning to others. That the raid was a success there was no doubt. The fires which had started even before we arrived had spread. Smoke had risen to 10,000 feet and the glow of the fires could be seen for at least the first 100 miles of the return journey. Later reports confirmed that the town centre had been devastated and industrial premises substantially damaged. However, the cost to Bomber Command was also substantial particularly to Group 1 (our Group). Out of a net 66 Lancasters which took off for the primary target, 9 were missing and 11 aircraft were more or less severely damaged. The blast of war had certainly blown in our ears.

I mentioned earlier that we had carried out low-level flying exercises. Taking these into account plus the low-level attack on Stettin and other subsequent training trips it could be that it was all part of a planned scheme to conceal the activities of Guy Gibson and his Dambusters, who were then training for their special operation in exactly four weeks time on the next full moon. Whatever the case, the month of April had ended and, as a crew, we had twelve completed operations to our credit. We had learned a lot but there was a great deal more to be learnt. We had probably only scratched the surface but perhaps deeply enough to realise that we couldn't take anything for granted.

SUMMARY FOR APRIL 1943

Date	Time	Aircraft	Pilot	Duty		Flying time
3	20.00	Lancaster W	Sgt Wells	Operations	ESSEN	4.45 hrs
4	20.30	" T	"	"	KIEL	5.30 "
8	21.50	" W	"	"	DUISBURG	5.00 "
9	21.00	" W	"	"	DUISBERG	4.00 "
13	20.50	" W	"	"	SPEZIA	10.00 "
18	21.00	" M	"	"	SPEZIA	9.25 "
20	21.40	" W	"	"	STETTIN	8.00 "

Although we did not realise it at the time, a really concentrated effort was being made to obliterate the industrial strength of the Ruhr. A moment's reflection would have indicated that the shorter nights in May and June would of necessity limit our activities to targets of no great distance and the Ruhr was the obvious answer. Is this the way the story would unfold? We shall see.

It was good news for the skipper who had been promoted to flight sergeant. This event coincided with the first trip of the month which was to be Dortmund. Unfortunately, our own Lancaster W could not be made serviceable in time so we would have to fly in a reserve aircraft. This was a blow, since we had grown fond of our own craft which had seen us through 8 operations and had withstood manfully the mauling received over Stettin. It was our thirteenth op and we were in for a shock since the Lancaster allocated was U-Uncle, which was thought to be the slowest (though not the oldest) deadbeat on the squadron. Not only was it slow, but it refused to fly above 17,000 feet – well below our accustomed operating height. Maurice in his cool and determined manner opted to press on regardless, knowing full well that the risks of being picked on by the German defences were proportionately higher. However, we were with 600 other aircraft on the largest non-1,000 bomber raid of the war, so it was unlikely that we would be alone even if we were near the bottom of the pile of Lancasters. All went well until we were half way over the heavily fortified zone . . . a sudden shout from Ray – Junker starboard beam . . . I swung round from port . . . he was right – slightly ahead and higher – he hadn't seen us . . . we fired simultaneously, and as we turned in, it dived and broke away underneath to the port bow and we did not see it again. Needless to say we continued to weave and follow an erratic course for some minutes afterwards. The better the weave the greater the comfort we used to say in our warped way. This brings me to a point which I could never understand or explain. When weaving, the skipper always claimed that his deviation either way was very positive. His contention was confirmed by another pilot, F/Sgt Rothwell, who accompanied us later on in the tour – yet to Ray and myself the motion was little more than being rocked gently in the cradle.

The raid on Dortmund was a success. The Group 1 report indicated that although there was a tendency for the attack to be slightly north of the target, by the end of the raid fires covered a very large area. It follows, of course, that where considerable fire activity has occurred there must also be an amount of bomb damage, since both high explosive and incendiary bombs were released at different times to ensure that they would land in a group, more or less in the same area. Apart from the explosions one could see during a raid, there was no way of telling immediately what damage the high explosive bombs had caused. However, it was later confirmed that the local steel factories had been extensively damaged, along with many other buildings. Civilian casualties were high and unfortunately a number of prisoners of war were also killed. Bomber Command's losses were slightly above average.

Due to the slowness of the aircraft we were late back to base and therefore stacked high over Wickenby waiting to land. So round and round we went losing height by 500 feet as each Lancaster ahead landed. Our turn seemed to take ages but eventually we landed and made our way through the normal processes to the debriefing room. I was first to enter and was spoken to by a good-looking chap, who was sitting behind a table just inside the door. He was wearing a flying jacket and I had therefore no idea of his rank or who he was. He asked me pleasantly how we had fared and I immediately replied, 'Well the XXXXXX kite wouldn't fly above 17,000 feet and was XXXXXXX slow.' 'Oh,' said he, 'I wonder why,' and then turned to Harry, who was following, to pursue his line of questioning, but obviously the latter was equally in an uncomplimentary mood. I forgot about this incident immediately but coincidentally or otherwise we did not fly in U-Uncle again and two operations later we were allocated Lancaster V-Victor. This aircraft was considered to be one of the fastest and highest Lancs in 12 Squadron. I sometimes wonder if this event, plus the fact that we were senior crew after not many operations and as such always flew in the first wave, might have been an important factor in successfully completing an operational tour.

Up to this point in my story I have not given much information about German night-fighters and other defence tactics employed by ground defences and what steps were taken in an effort to combat them. To Bomber Command crews, German night-fighters were a problem of the first order – a dangerous problem – and the odds of success were stacked in their favour. They had greater speed, fire power and manoeuvrability. As if this wasn't enough, they were also assisted by their ground 'box' system which effectively vectored them to the desired spot. The German Würzbung ground radar detectors gave information, which enabled the controllers to put night-fighters into the right positions to make interceptions. Again, the greatest problem was that the German night-fighter pilots were aware of the blind spot below British bombers generally, including Lancasters, and were able to use this to advantage. The amount of light at horizon level and above varied but a diligent gunner had a good chance of seeing a fighter approaching. However, unless there was 10/10ths cloud say at 10,000 feet and a little moonlight, it was very difficult to see anything in the murk below. Thus, on a moonless night it was an easy ploy for a fighter to slide underneath a bomber and fire (almost) at point blank range. Bomber Command had to live with this situation but a little assistance was obtained by partial jamming of German radar stations by a ground device in this country named 'Mandrel'. In addition, a microphone placed in one of the bomber's engines could be tuned by the wireless operator to any frequency on which he heard instructions being broadcast to German pilots.

Neither of these systems could cause a breakdown in the German defence but they could, at best, interrupt temporarily and, at worst, irritate their operators.

With high concentrations of bombers taking part in an air raid, an air gunner was aware, even on the darkest nights, of the presence of other craft within his vicinity. The question was were the 'black blobs' as they appeared from time to time, friend or foe? One became accustomed to concentrating one's sight slightly to the left or right of the 'blob' and ignoring direct vision. The eye, at night, can determine features more sharply away from the centre and this method was used to ascertain whether the object under scrutiny had four or two engines.* The latter would, of course, indicate the presence of a night-fighter ME 110 or JU 88, (although one had to be careful because at this period some twin-engined Wellington bombers were capable of flying at 20,000 feet). This system required a good deal of concentration but usually it was only for relatively short periods, since bombers did not bunch together for long spells due to several factors, but mainly because of the uncomfortable buffeting, which occurs when flying in the other chap's slipstream. Again, air crew were happier when not flying straight and level, and there was a tendency to weave as much as possible. This made life difficult for the navigator, of course, but even more so when a gunner asked for a search below and the pilot would blank steeply one way and then

---

* Because of the location of the optic nerve in the centre rear of the eye.

the other in an attempt to spot any fighter lurking in the gloom beneath. One method of taking evasive action was to 'corkscrew'. This manoeuvre called for the pilot to fly the plane on a horizontal spiral course. A moving target is always harder to hit and 'corkscrewing' was an effective counter attack either from the rear or underneath. However, it had to be used sparingly if rendezvous times were to be achieved.

Fighters were sometimes more active on the return route from the target. Because of this Maurice (termed a wise old owl by Harry), after diving away from and clear of the target area, then used to climb as high as possible. His theory was that it was safer to fly higher than the main body, since the German night-fighters would not wish to ascend any higher than necessary and it would be easier for their controllers. So, they would obviously settle for someone in the herd lower down. However, on one occasion, we were specifically instructed on leaving the Ruhr at 20,000 feet to fly straight and level for about 10 minutes then drop about 3,000 feet sharply – this ploy to be repeated until eventually crossing the Dutch coast at 5,000 feet. I had every reason to remember this tactic, since I had a heavy cold and I should have reported sick. But, of course, I had no wish to fall behind my colleagues in the number of operations completed and find at the end of their tour that I still had another trip to do which could well be with an inexperienced or scratch crew. This had to be avoided at all costs, so I said nothing and flew as normal. All went well until the first 3,000 foot descent occurred, when pressure built up in my ears and nasal passages and the pain became intense. Each time the manoeuvre was repeated the effect became worse due (I assume) to higher density of the atmosphere, so much so that, for the first time in my life, I was on the point of blacking out. I just managed to remain conscious fortunately, and was more than glad when the coast of Holland loomed into sight. Whether the tactics for the night were successful in keeping fighters at bay I know not but certainly this type of manoeuvre was not repeated again during the rest of the tour. I imagine, however, that the surprise element made for German control difficulties.

For certain we saw only four night-fighters during the tour but fortunately on each occasion none was in a position to attack. The odds were that at some stage or other we had been stalked but were, perhaps, lucky enough to avoid an attack by weaving just at the vital moment. As mentioned elsewhere, we had been selected three times for treatment by searchlights and it is therefore reasonable that, at least, on one occasion a fighter had been vectored on to our tail – but this must remain as pure speculation. On two occasions Ray and I were convinced that decoys were operating. An ever-changing coloured light appeared to be following us at level height on the starboard quarter. We took turns in watching this phenomenon while the other carefully searched the port quarter... Nothing happened and finally we concluded that we had been watching a setting planet (Venus was very bright during that period – I checked this with Patrick Moore the eminent astronomer, himself an ex-Bomber Command navigator). We had to take some leg-pull about this incident which had its lighter side but it brought to mind a passage from *Julius Caesar* I remembered from my schooldays which ran: 'Men at some time are masters of their fates: The fault, dear Brutus, is not in our stars but in ourselves...'

I have described previously how the German defences were able to trap bombers in searchlight cones by suddenly switching on a super-accurate master unit ably backed up by satellite units. There was no answer to this system where it existed but elsewhere it was fairly easy to prevent a single searchlight from fixing its target. The rule was to turn through the beam as it approached and then alter course again. This made it very difficult for the searchlight operator because of the relatively long delay in having to reverse his line of search and return to the point of contact. We proved this later in the war during mock air raids on London. It was hard work but for ten minutes or so we managed to evade being fixed and only gave up when the navigator's complaints became abusive. What happens in training, of course, is not necessarily a pattern for the real thing. One night we were routed home to the north of Aachen. We had been warned at briefing to keep away from this known heavily defended spot. On approach, a single searchlight probed from the north of our track but just too far away to turn through. The consensus of opinion was that we were slightly off track and possibly passing to the south of Aachen. It seemed advisable therefore to turn away from the searchlight which could be on the southern fringe of their defences. We did so and what a blunder! Seconds later on flicked the master searchlight to be followed shortly by the rest. We were well and truly coned again and the naked truth dawned on us. We must have been correctly on track to the north of Aachen and too far for the master searchlight to engage us effectively. The probing searchlight had nudged us over the spot of their choice. How their operations units must have laughed and slapped their thighs about these stupid British *Terrorfliegers* who had fallen into their trap. Fortunately their gunnery was not so efficient and we managed to escape unscathed. We learnt a lot from that experience, but perhaps Hippocrates had it right when he observed: 'How short the life, how hard the craft to learn.'

Chapter 12

Some Surprises

The tannoy crackled and blared out all over the station 'all operational crews to report to the briefing room at 14:00 hours'. At the due time we sat quietly in neat rows, crew by crew waiting for the vital question of our destination to be announced. Groans from the floor when the map revealed that we were to visit Duisburg for the fourth time in seven weeks. It seemed that we were being drawn by a magnet to this town. None wished to go to this target again which seemed rather silly, since all targets in the Ruhr were heavily defended, although Duisburg situated on the western perimeter should have required less penetration and should in theory have been an easier target – but not that anyone would notice.

It was difficult to explain this aversion to revisiting targets but, in a strange way, it may be related or similar to, the reason for people choosing different holiday locations year by year even though they may have enjoyed their last year's visit. The majority of people seem to feel that it is a mistake to revisit a resort, and there seems to be something in human nature which finds attraction in seeking pastures new. Come what may, Duisburg it was going to be, with a force of something near 600 aircraft. We would fly this time in Lancaster S-Swan, so termed in honour of its previous 'owner' Ken Swann. This plane was unique since it had the outline of a white swan painted below the pilot's window, plus an egg (instead of the usual bomb) for each operation completed. We were not to know it at the time, but in exactly one calendar month's time this aircraft would be lost in Dutch waters. It was found after the war when land reclamation operations were carried out at Dronten in Flevoland. When the town's local authority decided to erect a war memorial they incorporated one of S-Swan's propellers. Services are held there each Dutch Remembrance Day which are attended, amongst others, by representatives of the Air Gunners' Association. Eight streets in the new town were named in memory of the Lancaster and its last crew.

Duisburg was the raid on which I was suffering from a cold to which I referred to in the previous chapter, so I was in for a miserable night. To have a cold at ground level is one thing: it is quite another to try to blow one's nose in ultra-freezing conditions at 20,000 feet in a draughty turret, wearing an oxygen mask and using a frozen handkerchief containing abrasive ice crystals. To manoeuvre (fumble with is probably a better description) the mask and hanky when wearing three sets of gloves is a predicament which would only appeal to the humorous reflections of a low-class comedian.

Our bomb load, this time, took into account the fact that Duisburg is the largest inland port in Germany and was composed of 3 × 2,000 lb and 6 × 1,000 lb bombs. Unlike the three previous raids which were beset with weather problems, this time the conditions were nearly perfect and the Pathfinder Force had little difficulty planting their marker flares at the required spots accurately. The clear sky and exceptional visibility made Tommy's job easy and he responded by placing his bombs in the dock area, to the north of the city. Back at base, Maurice reported that he had observed four large explosions and that on leaving the target he had seen fires developing in an oblong shape running from north to south – coinciding with the required bombing run that night. He considered it to be a very successful raid and this subsequently proved to be the case. A considerable number of ships had been sunk or damaged and it would be some time before Duisburg would require the attention of Bomber Command again.

> Duisburg – four times we went there.
> N'er did we wish to – no sir, no sir.
> But this time we got it

Right in its eye socket
No need to revisit – Hallelujah!

Meanwhile, Chic had written to say that our old friend George, whom I had last seen at Cardington on day three of the war, had trained as a pilot in Texas, USA, and was now stationed at RAF Swinderby, about 10 miles south-west of Lincoln. I rang him and we arranged to meet in two days time provided 'Butch' Harris did not claim priority. George was now a flight lieutenant and had married Doreen, who was in the Waafs and was joining him that week-end on leave. He had started his operational tour a few weeks later than ours and with this and what happened in the intervening years, there would obviously be a lot to talk about. However, to cut a long story short, we met as arranged and having compared notes it turned out that we had both been on the Stettin and Spezia raids. Could we, without knowing it, have flown side by side over the Alps? It would have been a colossal coincidence but we will never be sure. No doubt we would have flown on further raids together, but George was having trouble with his legs and shortly afterwards it transpired that he was suffering from multiple sclerosis. He did not fly again and was discharged on medical grounds some months later.

The weather had entered a settled phase and it was no surprise when we were called to the briefing room after a few hours of fitful sleep. This time our venue would be Bochum, a fair-sized town situated in the heart of the Ruhr and concerned with the production of iron and steel. This was to be the main raid of the night involving some 450 aircraft. However, in addition (according to *the Bomber Command War Diaries*), a subsidiary force of Group 5 Lancasters would simultaneously attack the Skoda armaments factory at Pilsen but how they managed such a long trip during the shorter nights in May I cannot imagine.

It was later than 11p.m. as we waited on the end of the runway while Maurice ran through his final checks, first with Harry then each of us in turn. After each reported 'all clear' and a green light from the runway controller, off we rolled into the dusk after the skipper's 'here we go' . . . Take off was always a precarious moment especially with a heavy bomb load but the final thrust of power, which the Lancaster possessed, somehow seemed to convey a comfortable feel-

F/Lt Swan in the cockpit of S-Sugar. Note the distinctive swan insignia and eggs – one for each completed raid

The War Memorial at Dronden in Holland, this features a propeller of S-Sugar which crashed into the sea (before reclamation) on a site now occupied by the Town Hall which is shown in the background

ing that it would be able to lift the 3 × 2,000 lb and 5 × 1,000 lb bombs safely clear of the deck and onward to the lighter skies above. Visibility this night was very clear and the dark coastline of Norfolk, Lincolnshire and a goodly portion of Yorkshire stood out against the milky iridescence of the North Sea.

We set course for Bochum at around midnight at 20,000 feet with just a glimmer of light still showing on the port quarter but were conscious that this would disappear long before we reached the coast of Holland. So far so good. This was our first trip in our new Lancaster V-Vic. We thought our plane was the ex-flight commander's kite but subsequently it was established that this was not so. In fact our latest acquisition had just been delivered as brand new but no matter what, we were very proud of it. However, it seldom pays to be too sanguine in life ... something or someone will inevitably bring one down to earth. We had serenely and stealthily crept along towards Bochum to a point near the target when, for the third time, we were caught by searchlights. It was the usual routine – with deadly accuracy, on came the master searchlight, quickly followed by a huge battery of lights in support. Twisting and turning like a moth trapped in a street lamp, Maurice made his way towards the bombing point where he held V-Vic level long enough for Tommy to take aim. A vulnerable time this, which calls for a cool steady nerve when one feels like a sitting duck, if I may change the simile. With shells bursting all around us Tommy fastened his sights between two green ground markers before pressing the release button and announcing 'bombs gone'. The German artillery kept pounding away as we turned for home. Poor V-Vic was taking an awful bashing from flak or so it seemed. What a christening and a pity, since it was obviously in pristine condition on receipt. Inevitably we were losing height as we continued our crazy twisting flight but, seemingly after an age, the searchlights grew tired of us and, one by one, switched off to our great relief. We had been very lucky to have been caught in the centre of the Ruhr and escape without serious damage.

We were left in peaceful solitude for the rest of the night except for being shot at by the odd ship or two over the North Sea. This often happened. We complained time after time at debriefing about trigger-happy sailors but never received a satisfactory answer as to why we should play at being target practice for our own side. We blamed the Royal Navy for it but there was no proof. It could have been anyone. One possible cause could have been that our IFF (Indication Friend or Foe) was not switched on over the North Sea. This apparatus was activated when approaching the English coastline. Then along with the Verey lights giving the colours of the period, we could be identified as friendly, and the aircraft could be tracked back to base. It was because of these tracking problems that IFF could not be switched on over the sea since German night-fighter pilots would be able to home onto it with possible disastrous results. Without the means of identifying who was who, the RN were entitled to regard any passing aircraft as enemy. But this being the case, one would have thought that they would have been signalled in advance about RAF movements and not to fire on any aircraft during a given period, unless they were actively under attack.

Back at base we found that the damage to V-Vic was relatively light, just a few holes here and there which, at first sight, the ground crew thought could easily be repaired. Our early morning egg and bacon breakfast tasted unusually good but really we should have had champagne with it (that sounds an odd mixture – especially for early morning) since later we discovered that we had the best target photograph of the night. I should perhaps explain that, when the bomb aimer released his bombs, a photoflash pyrotechnical advice, housed in a chute under the mid-upper turret, was released also. This was set off by a pressure fuse to flash off above the bombing point and the plane's camera which had been similarly activated could thereby record the area bombed. I might add that I looked upon the large photoflash device with some disapproval – first the top corner of the chute acted as a step to climb-swing into the turret above, but one had to be very careful not to damage the protruding arming vanes of the photoflash. Secondly, in the event of an emergency in the dark it would become an unwanted impedance and, thirdly, in the event of fire it could become a menacing hazard. If it blew up I would, most likely, be blown out like a light – in a flash.

We tottered into bed at 8 am after two consecutive nights on the tiles hoping that we would have a spell of rest before the next onslaught. As it happened a period of ten days would elapse before we next operated – a most unusual break which had occurred only once before in March and, apart from spells of leave, would not happen again during the tour. Of course, we did not know what was coming. On the morning of 17 May we heard about the spectacular raid on the Mohne and Eder Dams by Wing Commander Gibson and his 617 Squadron Dambusters. To say that we were cheered by this event is an understatement – we were elated. It boosted our morale sky high and we felt as though we had just scored the winning goal in the World Cup Final, as presumably did the rest of the nation. It certainly was a major achievement by all concerned from Barnes Wallis onwards. We could never know, but it seems likely that the activities of Bomber Command were suspended until an assessment of the amount of damage to the Ruhr's industries caused by the Dambusters could be obtained.

Whatever the case, Bomber Command girded its loins and morale was still high when Dortmund was announced as the next target. There was always a different atmosphere when a big raid was in prospect. Everyone could feel the sense of occasion – a taking part in some enormously powerful and destructive project. The room was silent; faces of the briefing officers and crews were serious while the news that more than 800 aircraft would take part in the raid. There was no repartee during the briefing, at the end of which we filed out silently to make preparations. No sympathy was felt for the German population. Total war, in this age, affects everyone, the old, young, industrial workers, armed services and civilians alike. Man is a dangerous animal and when roused is capable of performing incredible acts which would be quite unthinkable in normal times. With the Dambusters raid still in our minds we had been aroused, invigorated and encouraged. With our colossal striking power we would press home our advantage.

Dortmund is a large city situated at the southern end of the Dortmund–Ems canal and an important industrial centre dealing in coal, iron, steel and machinery. Located at the west side of the Ruhr, it was a little more difficult to attack. We were to circumnavigate the Ruhr and approach from the north. The bomb load had been changed back to the more conventional 'cookie' and a mixture of incendiary bombs. The weather again was clear, no cloud and good visibility. No problems were encountered on the way to the target and on the bombing run Tommy had a great choice of aiming points. He chose the centre of two green markers which had been laid between two red markers. Our bombing run, which had been made at 18,000 feet on a heading of 160 degrees, seemed to indicate that everything was going right and that we were witnessing the beginning of another very successful raid. Indeed this turned out to be so. Large areas had been devastated, industrial plants damaged and a steel works demolished. It was significant that Dortmund was not raided again until the following year.

The complement of aircraft and personnel at RAF Wickenby had been increased and, during our period on operations, a third flight (C) had been added to 12 Squadron. This flight was intended to be the nucleus of a new 626 Squadron. It should have increased to full strength reasonably quickly but difficulties arose because losses were so high. My previous boss from RAF Aldergrove days, F/Lt Goudge, who had been flight controller was posted with his new crew to C Flight but was lost almost immediately. I was naturally somewhat shattered by this event. Later the new flight had to be temporarily disbanded and it was not until November 1943 that the new squadron became fully fledged and operational.

We did not discuss losses very much although we still had no real information – only hearsay and whatever information could be gleaned from the BBC news sources. However five per cent per raid appeared to be about right which accounted for the constant flow of new crews appearing in the sergeants' mess although a few familiar faces were to be seen on a daily basis for which we were glad. I never did see the mess humming with lively friendly activity which I had seen elsewhere but perhaps we had just gone through a bad period.

The weather which had been so favourable could not last and this we found to our cost on the next raid on Düsseldorf for which less than 800 bombers set out with the usual mixed load of bombs. On the way to the target most crews experienced problems with condensation trails. Generally we did not like 'contrails' as they were called, because they obviously indicated to a night-fighter pilot exactly the course and height of an individual aircraft and it was possible for him with his superior speed to 'sit' on the end and follow until within visual contact – in such conditions the German pilots had no need of radar or ground control instructions. For this reason Maurice sought to avoid contrails by altering height at intervals.

Another unusual (to me at least) condition that night caused lunar rainbows like giant hoops to appear to be encompassing both the horizontal and vertical axes of the plane with subsidiary circles appearing fore and aft. This phenomenon lasted for some 15 minutes in varying degrees of intensity and at one time other additional, but smaller, circles developed astern, ahead and on both beams horizontally plus one at the zenith. No doubt one would have appeared at the nadir had I been able to peer directly underneath. The whole show was as peculiar as it was spectacular.

Near the target, weather conditions were disappointing owing to cloud amounts which varied between 8/10ths to 10/10ths. Nevertheless, Tommy just managed to spot a green ground marker and bombed it. Although we may have been lucky it appeared that those following had run into worse conditions since Düsseldorf was not badly damaged apparently. It was generally regarded as a scattered raid which can usually be interpreted as a failure.

Life is full of surprises, so it is said. It certainly was true in the RAF especially in wartime conditions, as we were shortly to appreciate. Latish next morning we were idling in our hut when Maurice burst through the doorway. His usual calmness was perceptibly ruffled, when he announced that we were to change into 'best blue' and stand by. He had not been told the reason but in the words of Winco Woods – and I quote verbatim – 'no scarves with donkeys' heads on, or like apparel will be worn'. This gave rise to a good deal of speculation but no one could offer an explanation or even guess what might be in the offing. However, shortly we were told that we would be taken to our parent station at RAF Binbrook but still no reason was given for the trip.

We boarded a lorry and were joined by 'Mad' Macmillan and his Canadian crew. Mac had carried out fewer operations than ourselves but nevertheless was not far behind. He was as mystified as we were as to what was going on but it was no use speculating – the answer to the mystery would be revealed in due course.

Eventually we arrived at Binbrook and were all assembled in a large room together with crews from 100 and 460 Squadrons. We sat in neat rows facing the stage as we would be in a briefing and it was obvious that we were going to be addressed by someone. Eventually, the order to attention was given and onto the platform emerged the man I had last seen at Wickenby in the debriefing room. This time he was not wearing a flying jacket, his impressive row of medals, which included the VC, DSO, and DFC gave the clue. He was none other than Group Captain 'Hughie' Edwards – Station Commander of RAF Binbrook – I was somewhat abashed, when I realised how off-handedly, through unwittingly, I had spoken to this distinguished airman... But even more was I completely unprepared for his announcement that the King and Queen would shortly arrive at the station and each crew would be introduced to them.

As can be readily imagined all this caused quite a flutter amongst those present, which also included 'Laurie' Lawrence and his crew who had flown over from Wickenby. We were all quickly briefed on the current form of address to use, if spoken to, and were then assembled, crew by crew, on the forecourt of the officer's mess. Just before Their Majesties arrived 'Winco' Woods came along to Maurice and knowing him as a man of few words, and not wishing to have a breakdown of communications or an awkward silence at the vital moment of introduction, looked at him appealingly and whispered, 'For God's sake say something, Wells.' Not that in the event he had much need to worry, since the fire was taken out of the situation by Laurie Lawrence and his crew, who were presented immediately before us. They had had an unfortunate experience some four weeks previously (see page 168).

When returning from laying mines off Danzig they were attacked by a JU 88 and both gunners were badly wounded. Their aircraft had been badly damaged, they were obliged to land at RAF Coltishall and their gunners were taken to hospital. Their wireless operator had been more fortunate. An unexploded 20mm cannon shell had lodged in the hydraulic reservoir just above his head. This was recovered and eventually handed to their bomb aimer – F/Sgt Bert Cruse – a young Canadian from Winnipeg. On being introduced to Their Majesties by their skipper, Bert was holding the cannon shell and the Queen asked him how he came by it. After telling his story the Queen commented sympathetically, 'What a terrifying object,' to which Bert rejoined in his slow Canadian drawl, 'Yes Ma'am it certainly put the sh...' He paused and the Queen quickly interjected by replying, 'I can well imagine it did young man.' After this episode Maurice, although introduced, was not called upon to speak and only our Rhodesian wireless operator – Trevor – in his gentlemanly way needed to say a few well chosen words about his country and his peacetime occupation. Thus, perhaps, partially redressing the balance of respectability.

In the circumstances we could be forgiven if we thought that our experience was enough for one day. We were mistaken. Duty called us to the briefing room. This time it would be Essen – our third 'go' at this target. More than 500 aircraft would take part carrying the usual mixture of bombs. Since the cloud over the target was expected to vary between 8 to 10/10ths, instead of using ground markers PFF would place sky markers over the target. These flares burned with a steady but intensely red light and dripped green stars at regular intervals. They appeared to be suspended at 16,000 feet and when aimed at it was expected that the bombs would carry through to the chosen part of the target beneath. The sky markers could clearly be seen and the attack began. A rosy glow developed under the cloud which indicated that fires had started but whether these were at or near the intended target point it was impossible to say. One good feature of this and the previous raid was that searchlight and fighter activity had been curtailed and flak, although heavy at times, was largely ineffective. I was interested to see, in a Group 1 Summary, that a group liaison officer had been a passenger in one of the aircraft on the Düsseldorf raid. He described the flak as 'pitiful'. What this lull was due to, heaven knows, but it was safe to assume that it wouldn't last.

So, operations for the month ended in a lower key but it was time for leave again and with indecent haste the crew split up and went their various ways.

SUMMARY FOR MAY 1943

Date	Time	Aircraft	Pilot	Duty	Flying time	
4	22.00	Lancaster U	F/Sgt Wells	Operations	DORTMUND	5.00 hrs
12	23.30	" S	"	"	DUISBURG	4.45 "
13	23.15	" V	"	"	BOCHUM	5.40 "
23	22.15	" V	"	"	DORTMUND	5.15 "
25	23.45	" V	"	"	DÜSSELDORF	4.00 "
27	22.30	" V	"	"	ESSEN	4.45 "

THE TURRETS OF WAR

Sgt McMillan (dark glasses) and (scratch) crew

"Laurie" Lawrence and his crew

The King and Queen larking informally to representative aircrews of 12,100 and 460 squadrons outside the officer's mess at RAF Binbrook, May 1943

Chapter 13

The (Un)happy Valley

Maurice had become friendly with a family in Norfolk. They owned a farmhouse situated in the middle of nowhere and this was just the job for the skipper who, I am sure, was a countryman at heart. The two Rhodesians made for London, which was the social centre for most Commonwealth service personnel. Joe made for his home in Darlington; Harry to his beloved Blackpool; Tommy to Leicester and myself to Sunderland where, along with Chic and Bowie, we made our way nostalgically to Ambleside, to be welcomed warmly by the homely owner of Rothay Home Cottage. What a journey; it took longer, I contemplated, to travel the 100 miles, or so, cross-country than it took to fly to Spezia, bomb and return to base. However, this was no time to mull over the events of the last few weeks. We were free to roam in a peaceful sane world, amongst the Lake District hills and scenery which we had found so delightful pre-war.

Some of my earliest memories as a child concerned Cumbria. I remember being driven along the road high above the west side of Lake Derwentwater in a charabanc and the argument which ensued after our driver had 'carved-up' a horse drawn carriage causing damage to both vehicles; also holidays in Keswick where by repute my grandfather, a Presbyterian parson, had climbed Skiddaw dressed in his pastoral clothing including his high-silk hat. He loved the hills and had passed on this love to the rest of the family. As a boy I was attracted to them. Using YHA facilities I explored them by push-bike and on foot in blistering heat and pouring rain alike. I felt at home in their environment. Later during our courting days Chic and I laboured up Dungeon Ghyll Force to Harrison Stickle, the highest of the Langdale Pikes; up Rosset Gill by Esk House to Scarfell Pike; sweated up Styhead Pass, across the Climbers' Traverse and up the boulder-strewn Little Hell Gap to the top of Great Gable; romped over Striding Edge, carrying our five-stone Labrador dog, Donnie, down the last forty-feet drop before making the final easy ascent to the summit of Helvellyn and returning by Swirrel Edge to Patterdale. They were happy magical days.

I recall one fine evening in September when Chic and I were scree-running down the west side of Great Gable at sunset. To the west lay Wastwater lake which, due to the vast screes on its south side, often looked drab and desolate but now the setting sun floodlit the lake which gleamed with ever deepening colours ranging from orange to red. The colours were taken on, in turn, by the screes and valley; to the sea beyond and the sky. The whole scene was aglow. A vast coalescence of the elements radiantly reflecting the deepening sunset hues. A panoramic spectacle which only nature can produce. We sat down; the air was still; the sun and rocks were still pleasantly warm and the colourful scene was there to savour. We sat in silence, close together, hand-in-hand and watched until the deepest red hues faded – at peace with the world. Forty years would pass before we would enjoy a similar experience but this time 7,000 miles away in Arizona, with the sun setting over the Grand Canyon . . . But quickly, quickly! we were still about 2,000 feet up and the light would not last much longer. We would have to run the screes as never before – we did, leaving a trail of dust and loose stones clattering down in our wake. Our tough-nailed mountain boots stood up to the rough treatment and fortunately neither of us fell back onto our elbows or other unmentionable parts of our bodies. This could be quite a painful hazard when sliding and skidding down loose scree. We had descended the first 1,000 feet in about ten minutes, but now could see where we had left our car in the valley below and we ran (perhaps bounded would be a better description) easily over the smooth springy turf on the lower slopes of Gable to reach it just before darkness fell.

Ah well, such happy days could not last for ever, yet here we were in the same locality but much restricted in our activity by our infant daughter and lack of transport. Nevertheless, as a small family group we had had little time together to enjoy each other's company and now the opportunity had arisen we must use it to the full, hour by hour, day by day. We managed to walk to Rydal Water, and would have liked to have visited a favourite spot of ours at the top of Red Bank with its outstanding view over Grasmere, backed by Dunmail Raise and Helvellyn but it was too far. We did visit Skelwith Bridge and made our way sufficiently far into Langdale Valley to gaze around the familiar scenery wistfully. We admired the excellent example of a U-shaped glaciated valley as we sat paddling our feet in the cool waters of Langdale Beck, under the shadow, as it were, of Bow Fell, Crinkle Crags and The Pikes. At the head of the valley above the terminal moraine we could see the start of walks which could lead one on to the highest hills. Would we ever have the opportunity to don our boots and rucksacks again and repeat the experiences of our pre-war days? Only time would tell.

The leave period was nearly over and it was time to return to Sunderland for a short stay, before travelling back to Lincoln. Partings with one's family during wartime were always difficult and had to be faced with a grin and a cheery wave covering suppressed emotions. All servicemen had to contend with this but, fortunately, the trains were crowded with uniforms, cigarette smoke and people of every description and a very helpful spirit prevailed – very un-British by peacetime standards but it helped a lot to while away time spent on long irksome journeys.

I arrived back at Lincoln around 6.30 p.m. There was no transport back to camp until 10 p.m. so the nearest cinema seemed to be the best solution. Ronald Coleman and Greer Garson were appearing in *Random Harvest*. This was an excellent film (it still is) by any standards but highly emotional and a tugger of heart-strings. It was totally unsuitable for an end of leave entertainment and I can tell you that it was a very lonely and dejected airman who returned to Wickenby that night.

The crew had assembled. Yes ... we had all had a smashing time. Wacko this and wacko that in the accepted parlance of the period. We each had a grossly exaggerated story to tell and we laughed over these and about the time Harry arrived back late from Lincoln one night to find the hut full of smoke. Tommy had gone to sleep leaving a lighted cigarette on his biscuit (a service name for a mattress) which was merrily smouldering away. Harry, always claimed that he had saved our lives by prompt action and exemplary devotion to duty. Photographs were taken of the crew outside the hut but alas, when developed, they were all found to be out of focus. Something had gone wrong with the camera's mechanism – or so it was said.

The crew was ready to do its stuff again. To carry on this strange double life – a mixture of normal and abnormal. A peaceful, almost mundane existence changing suddenly into a vicious battle of modern technology in which the contestants had no personal contact. To the German night-fighter pilots and artillery teams the only thing that mattered was to dispose of that threatening object in the sky. The human element contained therein was of no consequence. Similarly, our bomb loads were delivered as planned, but as the aircraft lurched on release of the lethal dose no thought was given to those on the receiving end. A sense of detachment made all things possible and even the scene over the target with its fairyland setting of pretty lights, more akin to a giant fireworks display, gave rise to a feeling of unreality. Had Walt Disney designed such a scenic spectacular it surely would have been acclaimed universally.

However, the time for reality arrived when the tannoy indicated that our presence was required in the briefing room at 15.00 hours. So it was back to business again and although we now had eighteen operations to our credit it was too early to think in terms of completing the tour which could take anything up to two months. It was better to concentrate on the present situation and on the way to the 'genhouse', as it was known, we had little doubt about the area we would next be required to visit. The target could surely be no other than in the Ruhr.

Our prognosis was soon confirmed. The target would be Oberhausen, one of the smaller towns lying between Duisburg and Essen. The very sound of these two names indicated that there would be strong opposition but, worse that this, the weather forecast was for varying degrees of cloud cover up to 10/10ths at 10,000 feet and a bright moon. We would easily be spotted by fighters from above. By the same token, of course, we would also be able to observe an intending attacker more easily from below. Height would be an important factor and in this respect we were lucky since V-Vic was good at showing the others the way up. Despite this there would be a great need for vigilance. More so, because fewer than 200 Lancasters would be taking part and the safety-in-numbers factor would be reduced.

A small bomber force for a small town, we thought, less than 180,000 population and just about the same size as my hometown, although this did not strike me at the time. I try to imagine what sort of damage would have occurred at home if, say, 900 tons of bombs had been dropped in one night. I shudder to think of the consequences and conclude that had the bombs been dropped in a fairly even pattern on the parts of the town that mattered, enormous damage would have been done to vital industry. As it was, Sunderland appeared amongst the seven most bombed towns in the country (so it was claimed). I could not obtain firm figures about the actual total tonnage of bombs dropped locally by the Luftwaffe but it seems likely that Bomber Command were about to deliver, in a single night, a much greater weight of bombs than Sunderland received all during the war. This perhaps helps to put the matter into perspective.

Due to the fact that the target would be cloud covered, the Pathfinders planned to place sky markers at the appropriate spot by using OBOE again. So off we went carrying the usual load. The weather forecasters had done their job well. A thin layer of cloud covered the area ghostly white in the bright clear moonlight. The sky markers stood out brilliantly as we bombed on 023 degrees from a height of 21,000 feet. We turned for home and Maurice seemed confident that this deliberate blind bombing attack had been successful. Fires could be seen glowing through the cloud and even Ray, who rarely commented, was more than vociferous as we were leaving the target.

Subsequent reports confirmed that a good deal of damage had been sustained by Oberhausen but the cost to Bomber Command had been relatively high with the loss of 17 Lancasters – nearly nine per cent of the bombing force.

In training for operational flying, much importance was attached to parachute drill and what to do in the unfortunate event of having to bale out over enemy territory. One question uppermost in my mind was never answered. Imagine flying over the target area at say 15,000 to 20,000 feet and receiving an order to abandon aircraft.

Assuming that you were able to combat G forces, which can be high if the aircraft is in a tail-spin: that, in the darkness, you can find your parachute and clip it on to your harness: that you can find and unfasten the door or hatch and dive out without being hit by some projection on the aircraft, then you are free to decide when to pull the 'string' which will release the parachute. Easy? Yes but there is a snag or two. You must then decide whether to:

Pull the rip-cord straight away and risk the possibility of being struck by another bomber or a shower of incendiary bombs or shrapnel from artillery fire, in the hope that the wind would carry you away from the target area into open country thus giving a better chance of landing unseen and thereby increasing the chance of escape, OR

Delay pulling the rip-cord until, say 5,000 feet (if you can judge it) thus avoiding some of the hazards in the first option but instead having to risk the possibility of landing in the target area and being bombed or having to face the wrath of a howling mob of mixed ARP personnel, police, firemen or civilians who might not be under cover. In any event, most raids were over in thirty minutes which is not long enough in an urban area to escape before people would emerge from their shelters.

What would you have done, apart from praying? You tell me, I can almost hear you say... Well, I don't think I will ever know the answer but I sometimes wonder if another overriding factor might have settled the issue. I can imagine that on falling through the air at increasing speed, one's first thoughts would concentrate on whether the parachute would open correctly. If so, cool thinking and a careful weighing up of all the factors involved in the prevailing conditions might have gone by the board and one would have instinctively pulled the string. Assuming the parachute opened, the issue would have been settled and the first option would apply.

Fortunately, I never did have to make such a decision, but it certainly gave much food for thought at the time. Being shot down and having to escape was always a possibility which one might encounter. We were well equipped for such an event having been provided with a small escape pack, which included items such as Horlicks tablets, a tube of condensed milk, a small bar of chocolate (part of one's rations), a water bag with chlorine tablets, matches and adrenalin tablets for use if being pursued or in a tight corner. We carried the currency of each country to be overflown and were provided with our photographs in civilian clothing which would be needed for a passport or identity papers by the underground resistance organisations if they could be contacted. We did not carry any personal papers or letters or indeed any unnecessary object which could help a German interrogator, if caught. Finally, we were provided with compasses of a type which could be concealed on the person. A button or pencil clip, for example. These, to my mind were not so important since on a cloudless night a sight of the Pole Star would suffice and, by day, the sun's position or the mossy side of trees or their direction of lean would normally provide the answer. All this assumed that one would be in a fit state to travel but, if all was well, the first action to take after landing was to conceal the parachute and harness – not an easy task at night and in open country – and then make as much distance as possible from the landing point before daylight. Thereafter, it was a matter of survival by using one's wits and initiative; or animal cunning and thieving or just relying on plain luck. Obviously, no special information could be given on how to contact the resistance movement with the exception that if one could make the distance to Paris and then hang about the Gard du Nord, eventually, if luck held, the right people would be contacted. Many shot down air crew managed to return home by various means and I am sure that many good stories remain untold but I am glad I have no such personal tale to relate.

The night following it was the turn of Cologne to become the target. Again a force of less that 200 bombers would be operating and the raid was planned to commence at 0103 and finish at 0120 – a tight schedule. Cologne had a population of about 500,000 so bang went the small-target-small-force theory. We had not visited this city before, although we had been close to it from time to time. Apocryphal, or otherwise, a gap in the heavily defended zone was supposed to exist between Cologne and Düsseldorf slightly to the north. We had been routed through this 'gap' on a few occasions but had never noticed that the German flak activity was any less. On the contrary we seemed to receive a peppering from both sides. It would therefore be interesting to discover what Cologne had to offer, on its own, when we approached. In the event, no discernible difference was apparent. On the other hand, conditions were not good. Cloud up to 25,000 feet, with occasional lightning flashes had been observed on the way over and the target was obscured by 10/10ths cloud with tops up to 15,000 feet. Sky markers were in operation again and it seemed doubtful if a satisfactory outcome would be achieved. However, a following reconnaissance indicated to the contrary so, with this evidence and that of previous raids, where sky marking had been used, it seemed that this method was not as hit-and-miss as one might have supposed. Again, with a small raid, the loss to Bomber Command was higher than average.

V-Vic was behaving herself well. We had bombed Cologne from a height of 23,000 feet, the highest yet in our experience, and normally we had no trouble in arriving home in the first batch and sometimes in the premier position. This was always an advantage. No waiting in a queue to land, no waiting for transport at dispersal. No queue for debriefing and, most important of all, no queue for breakfast. In consequences of all this, one would be able to roll into bed a lot earlier than would otherwise be the case. Sleeping well is not easy when one's regular hours are upset and this happened often during the heavier operating periods.

We were all out of bed about mid-day when the door opened and a member of our ground maintenance crew appeared. He was a bright cheery fellow. I cannot remember his name or trade but he stood in the doorway rather hesitantly and a trifle sheepish. 'Wat'cher want mate?' was the obvious question put and the answer came quickly. He would like to go on an 'op' with us. Cor! We were impressed by his spirit and by the fact that he had enough faith in us to see him through. We could have laughed him out of it, but no, this was a serious request and deserved due consideration. He was obviously motivated by a desire to see for himself exactly what a bombing mission was like and was willing to risk his neck. He could act as another pair of eyes by standing in the astrodome and watch for night-fighters, thereby earning his keep. Fine, but had he thought of what might happen if he and we were shot down? Even at best, as a prisoner of war he could face a court martial on return and, although we might be able to borrow some necessary equipment for him such as a helmet and intercom etc, it was very questionable as to how a parachute and harness could be obtained. Even if we could, he had received no parachute or emergency training or ditching drill. All in all therefore, it was better for him (and us) to drop the idea. The last word, of course, was with the skipper who had presided over the foregoing. His answer was in the negative. I don't blame him. He, personally, would have been on a hiding to nothing had he been discovered conniving with the request even to the point of being court martialled. Really it was the only possible answer to give, even though we (and, I suspect he) would have liked to have obliged this keen and interested airman. I have no evidence of unauthorised passengers having taken part on 'ops' but I'd be willing to bet that somewhere, somehow, someone managed to do it. For certain it was not possible for anyone to hide in a Lancaster prior to take off and then suddenly announce 'yoo-hoo I'm here' when half way over the North Sea and too late to turn back.

Night-flying tests (NFTs) were carried out usually, but not always, before each operation. The skipper had discretion as to the length of the test and where we should go in order to ascertain, as far as possible, that the machine (and its attendant equipment) was fully serviceable. Often we would fly over Lincolnshire to The Wash and fire our guns out to sea, blazing away merrily at some unseen enemy, or firing on the beam and watching the antics of precessing tracer bullets.* Browning machine guns were fairly reliable but they did tend to freeze up in unfavourable conditions and suffer from stoppages for other reasons. Often a fault could be cleared by recocking and firing again, which is just as well because although we were all skilled in diagnosing faults and how to rectify them, in combat conditions it was impossible to do much. The mechanical action of these weapons was too complicated. Imagine for instance, having five or ten seconds to rectify a fault in a car's distributor in complete darkness wearing three sets of gloves (silk, electrically heated and leather). Fortunately on the three occasions I fired my guns in anger, they did work. Careful and methodical maintenance on the ground could not guarantee a hundred per cent

---

* Analogously like a spinning top whereby the wobble of a spinning object causes its axis of rotation to become cone shaped.

success but at least it reduced greatly the possibility of failure at the vital time.

NFTs were a good opportunity for Maurice to practise his low-level flying skill. His favourite trip was to the farmhouse in Norfolk. He would skim over the fields so low that the slipstream of each engine could easily be seen creating channels in the tops of wheat fields. He would fly at great speed aiming at the poplar-screened farmhouse and at the last moment, pull the nose up just in time to clear the roof. The occupants turned out bravely to acknowledge the salute by waving sheets or blankets as we shot over. He would repeat the process three times and each 'woosh' seemed closer. The mid-upper position is the best all-round viewing position on the aircraft and there were times when I wondered whether we would survive another shoot-up (I am a bad back-seat driver). I wondered too how Maurice got away without being taken to task for unauthorised low flying but, as he pointed out in later correspondence to me, it is very difficult to identify markings on low-flying aircraft. People are usually taken by surprise. One doesn't hear a plane approach at low level until it is almost overhead and away, so one doesn't have time to take the number or marking details, even if one knows where to look...

But the Daddy of all these adventures happened when we were in the Blackpool area. Harry wished to see his tower from the air. Maurice obliged... We swept in low from the sea and with our huge black monster, did the tightest possible turn around and below the top of the tower. The consternation could easily be seen on the faces of those on the promenade below and Maurice later observed that this was also reflected by Harry's face as we flew round at an incredible angle, only 200 feet up.

There was another incident, before I joined the crew, when they were flying over the sea off Scarborough. Maurice wished to see how low he could fly over the unusually calm water and he had the rear gunner, Ray, looking down from the rear turret to tell him when the sea was rippled by the propellers slipstreams. Ah well, who doesn't do foolish things when young but, who knows, the skill and judgement he acquired by these escapades may have paid off on the Stettin raid.

The skipper's flying ability was never in doubt by any member of

F/Lt Maurice Wells DFM taken in 1945

the crew. All of us would go anywhere with him. He seemed at home with and enjoyed controlling this twenty-nine ton mass of complicated machinery. Even when practising flying with two port or starboard engines feathered (inoperative) and changing directions by turning into them he did not appear to be in any difficulty, and every mid-upper gunner knows just how dicey it seems looking down the length of the wing at the ground over two dead engines. His landings were always smooth and in those more polite days he deserved the accolade of 'nice one Maurice' voiced usually by Trevor over the intercom immediately after touchdown. Only once, in my experience, was he in any difficulty when, for some reason which now escapes me, he attempted to land without the flight engineer's assistance in following up the engine controls. This resulted in an enormous bounce and a rough second, third and perhaps fourth contact with the runway. In exceptional circumstances there was no criticism. Only wide grins.

We were lazily sprawled outside our hut enjoying the warm June sunshine when the tannoy reminded us that 'Butch' Harris was beckoning. Where now? It just had to be the Ruhr. It was. The red line on the briefing-room map ran over the Dutch coast to Krefeld which lies in the south-east corner of the Happy Valley. Its industries were mixed, covering such items as steel, chemicals and textiles. Its size was similar to Oberhausen which had sustained a good deal of damage a few nights earlier but the ominous difference was that this time more than 700 aircraft were expected to take part – thus tripling the effort. If bombing accuracy and concentration could be achieved the outcome would be horrific.

For this raid we would carry a 'cookie', 3 x 500lb HE bombs and 48 x 30lb plus 30 x 41lb incendiary bombs – an unusual combination. It was a peaceful, warm summer's evening when the transport dropped us at dispersal and left us to sort out our gear. Time enough to play football with a few stones lying around or indulge in boyish horseplay? No fear! Ray and I, and to some extent Tommy, had to keep ourselves as cool as possible. There was no point in making our socks and underwear damp with sweat. This would only lead to extremely uncomfortable and chilly conditions, even to the extent of frostbite sometimes, at 20,000 feet. Rear gunners were equipped with full-length, electrically heated suits but mid-upper gunners, for some peculiar reason, were only supplied with electrically-heated jackets which had connections down the back of each leg to heated socks. Despite the electrically heated gloves, my hands were sometimes very cold but nearly always my legs from the knees downwards and feet felt frozen due to the draughts blowing down the fuselage which searched through the layers of my (supposed) windproof flying suit, trousers, socks, electrically heated socks and flying boots. One ingenious wag suggested that I should wear cricket pads on the back of my legs. I might just have tried this if a pair had been available but I would have looked an odd spectacle if I'd had to bale out over Germany. Doubtlessly my appearance would have astonished the Huns!

Maurice wanted to be off in order to be nearer the head of the queue. We were some distance away from the main runway and on a warm night such as this engines could easily overheat before take off and there was no point in having to scrub an 'op' on this account. So, in we popped, stowed parachutes, checked this and that, including hatches, and waited for Maurice to start up. Each engine burst into life with a puff of exhaust and a roar and then a pause for each to be run-up while checks were made. This completed, chocks away and off we went around the perimeter to the main runway. There was already activity over the Lincolnshire countryside as we took off and this increased substantially as we climbed and then dog-legged, in an effort to waste time, until the precise moment arrived to set course.

At the enemy coast, searchlight cones were active over Amsterdam and Rotterdam as usual. Those cones were nearly always in evidence in Ruhr raids and this was no exception. Our route seldom took us close to either of these localities and often I used to wonder why their searchlights were so consistently in use. I never did discover the answer but it seems likely that either diversionary raid planes may have been active or perhaps British night-fighters sent in to harass the German fighter bases may have been responsible.

With the coastline disappearing to the rear we were not bothered by enemy action but an occasional judder from the turbulence of those ahead was strangely comforting. After only 20 minutes or so we could see that activity was increasing over the Ruhr towns with the usual barrage well in evidence. The weather was almost perfect, practically cloudless *en route*. There would be no difficulties in finding the Pathfinders' target indicators on this occasion. Everything appeared right and, even as we came up to the target, the raid had that 'big prang' look about it. We bombed on 139 degrees from 20,000 feet. To describe the scene I cannot do better than to quote the brief report Maurice gave to the intelligence officer on return to base:

'No cloud. Visibility good. Red target indicators right on time many concentrated fires around markers. Pathfinders bang on. A very concentrated raid.'

As usual we had bombed early with the first wave but even as we turned for home the town had become a seething mass of flames and these could be seen as far away as the coast. Krefeld had suffered a holocaust. As a result of researches after the war, Martin Middlebrook and Chris Everitt in their book gave the following account:

> ... the Pathfinders produced an almost perfect marking effort, ground markers dropped by OBOE Mosquitoes being well backed up by the Pathfinder heavies (ie Halifaxes etc) 619 aircraft bombed these markers, more than three-quarters of them achieving bombing photographs within three miles of the centre of Krefeld. 2,306 tons of bombs were dropped. A large area of fire became established and raged, out of control for several hours. The whole centre of the city – approximately 47 per cent of the built-up area – was burnt out. The total of 5,517 houses destroyed, quoted in Krefeld's records was the largest figure so far in the war. 1,056 people were killed and 4,550 were injured. 72,000 people lost their homes ...*

Poor Krefeld – it had been bombed into a raging hell but the cost to Bomber Command had also been heavy with a loss of 44 aircraft – 6.3 per cent of the force ... War is no game for the faint hearted.

Next day (I should really say later the same day, of course, but you know what I mean), we had only just tumbled out of bed when it was announced that we were on ops again.

This time another of the smaller Ruhr towns was due for a pounding. In all 550 aircraft were detailed for a raid on Mulheim which was an even smaller locality than Krefeld. The weather was set fair and it looked as though we were in for a repetition of the previous night's experience. Our bomb load was the same, visibility would be good

* The Bomber Command War Diaries.

with no cloud *en route* or over the target. The stage was set and the curtains were due to be raised on another scene of horror.

On the way to the target we saw Krefeld was still burning. It appeared as a large oval mound of red embers like a giant' bonfire dying down. This description is not mine but taken from a Group 1 Summary for that night. I quote it because it so accurately describes the scene which is indelibly imprinted on my memory. I cannot do better.

'The raid on Mulheim went as planned. The target was approached and bombed on 170 degrees at 20,000 feet. Again, Maurice reported at debriefing that we had bombed through thin broken strato-cumulus cloud on red markers placed dead on time and which were surrounded by concentrated fires. He added that he had seen a number of explosions on leaving. This brief statement was really his way of saying that the raid had indeed been a carbon copy of the previous night's débâcle but again at heavy cost – the loss of 35 aircraft or 6.3 per cent.'

We turned for home and as we proceeded it was difficult not to let one's eyes stray back to the glow of the burning target which could easily be seen from the Dutch coast. There was a danger here of loss of vigilance which could be fatal and it was vital to maintain concentration.

However, no difficulties were encountered on the return journey and we had a smooth flight back to base. From the Dutch coast onwards over the North Sea, with nose slightly down the flight gave one an opulent feeling brought about by a silent and smooth passage through the air as though we were gliding. After all we had 20,000 feet plus to lose in less than 90 minutes.

That night the High Command had pity for us and we were given a rest – but only for a short while, because the next day the tannoy crackled its woeful message.

The Ruhr again? Yes, but this time the map track took us through the mythical gap between Cologne and Düsseldorf. We were going to have to run the gauntlet again and then push on to Wuppertal which would be the target for the night. A quite large town this – a conurbation really – positioned in the south-east of the Ruhr. It had various industries which included textiles, leather and rubber goods. This locality had been bombed heavily during the last time we were on leave and was now to be given another go.

The weather was still holding, though the possibility of haze and thin cloud existed. All went well until our time to go through the 'gap' arrived. The flak seemed heavier than usual and we wondered if, in view of recent activity, the Germans had brought up reserves from elsewhere. There was a limit to what they could afford to do in this direction, on which I comment later, but the Germans were not noted militarily for letting the grass grow under their feet. Once through the 'gap' we very quickly arrived over Wuppertal. There was a little ground haze over the target, but not enough to obscure the Pathfinder markers. Maurice, however, found a layer of 10/10ths strato-cumulus cloud at 19,000 to 21,000 feet and was obliged to descend to 18,500 feet. We were not the first on the target by any means and, on arrival, fires were going well. Wuppertal lies in a narrow valley and the fires had already started to illuminate both sides – the tree-lined hills stood out clearly. Tommy had no difficult in selecting a red ground marker and, after 'bombs away', we continued to fly roughly NE by E up the valley, before eventually turning for home. Maurice's comments at debriefing on the night's work were 'the whole place seemed to be one sheet of flame. Best attack I have ever seen'. I later noticed that he had the distinction of thus being quoted in the Group 1 Summary of Operations for that night.

As we left the target, smoke was beginning to drift upwards and later arrivals reported that this eventually rose to 17,000 feet and covered the whole valley, which must have made bombing difficult for them.

We had become accustomed to seeing urban areas glowing as we proceeded home and this night was no exception, although unexpectedly it could not be seen from the coast. It was assumed to be due to the screening effect of the surrounding valley and the smoke barrier above. Nevertheless, it was obvious that we had witnessed another colossal disaster for the Germans. On the other hand, Bomber Command had suffered in proportion. Out of the 630 aircraft dispatched 34 had been lost – 5.4 per cent of the force. This made a total loss of 113 aircraft during the last three raids – a very heavy price to pay.

Back at base and through the usual procedures, we were off to bed by 6 a.m., only to find at lunch time that we were 'on' again . . . Crumbs – four operations in five nights. This was really really rubbing it in. It was not only pressure on operational crews, the whole station must have been working at full steam, especially the maintenance crews. However, no grumbles were heard, no dissension, no groans, moans or what-have-you. Staff worked any hour of the day or night as required and remained cheerful. Certainly we were lucky in having good leadership in 'B' Flight. Two flight commanders were in post during the period of our tour: Squadron Leader D H Villiers initially and his successor Squadron leader A J Heyworth. During the time that I was seeking information on various aspects of this book I became aware of facts that I had not known previously about the service background and philosophy of the latter and how he was so well fitted for the job in hand. For example, he had seen a lot of action even from his earliest days when under training. During his first solo flight at night, in an Anson near Little Rissington, a JU 88 'shot up' the airfield and bombed the runway. He had to circle round with no lights for 30 minutes whilst below they repositioned the flare path to run between two bomb craters. In due course the chance light was switched on then went out again but eventually he landed by the light of flares alone ... He was then aged 18!

Twelve Squadron had been equipped with Fairy battle aircraft at the onset of the war but after returning from France they converted to Wellington Mk IIs. It was as this juncture, in June 1941, that Jim Heyworth joined the squadron and then went on to complete his first operational tour by February 1942. In so doing he gained the distinction of being the first pilot to complete 30 operational sorties on 12 Squadron since the beginning of the war ... I was astonished by this revelation, but it was a pointer to the hazardous state of operational flying in the early days. He certainly deserved to be 'screened' from active squadron duties for a spell.

On his return to 12 Squadron for a second tour, David Villiers was his flight commander for a few days before being posted. In that short time he felt the latter's aura of charm and appreciated his undoubted qualities of leadership. On takeover, Jim Heyworth believed that there were two necessary objectives – to instil confidence into the flying crews, especially those starting their first tour of operations, and to ensure the thorough maintenance of aircraft.

That air crew should have aircraft they could trust was paramount but it was a problem not easily solved. The ground engineers were given almost impossible targets of reliability to meet, yet they consistently produced 80 to 90 per cent serviceability. It was significant that when not on operations himself JH, as he was known, used to visit dispersal huts to keep their spirits up and show appreciation for their careful maintenance, this and like action was obviously the right sort of approach.

To have control of ten crews and a team of engineers would, I imagine, be regarded as an onerous task in peacetime conditions but in wartime with shortages, the need to improvise and operational pressures, it must have been daunting. He had certainly been saddled with an enormous responsibility early in life . . . at only 22 years of age.

Well, so much for behind the scenes. Where next would the briefing room map reveal? The answer was Gelsenkirchen. Few seemed to have heard of it before although we should have, since it was a fairly sizeable town dealing with the usual hardware and chemicals but, more importantly, it had a plant for producing synthetic oil. It had received the attention of Bomber Command on a regular basis earlier in the war, but it had not been a prime target for about two years. The bomb load was the same as before but, unlike the previous three raids, the weather was likely to be cloudy. It certainly was – 10/10ths cloud with tops up to 10,000 feet and, for some reason or other, the Mosquito Pathfinders failed to place their markers correctly and were late. Considerable fire glow appeared under the cloud but it was too early to be sure of anything. In fact, as had happened on some previous occasions, the raid had become scattered and there was no concentration of effort over Gelsenkirchen. So, we had wasted our time and resources for very little return, but there was another angle to it that night. We were accompanied by F/Lt J N Roland. The reasons for his presence were not known, but the skipper thought he might have been a reporter or an intelligence officer. Whether he was either of these is speculative but, obviously, a poor example of Bomber Command's activity was all we had to offer on the night.

Again the losses were high. According to Bomber Command, 30 aircraft were missing out of 473 dispatched. This, superficially, represented a 6.3 per cent loss but it seems unlikely that the actual percentage loss would be much higher since, usually, the number of aircraft dispatched is a gross figure. It does not take into account the number of those who aborted for various reasons and returned to base, having not taken part in the raid.

We encountered no problems on the return journey from Gelsenkirchen except that over the North Sea we were shot at by a ship – again. But as the English coastline hove into view the best part of the night's proceedings were to come. It was always a comfort to hear, over the intercom, the words 'IFF on' and then turn to watch the colours of the day being fired by Trevor from the launching position near the top of the fuselage forward of the mid-upper turret, also to hear Maurice call base, PINTO V-VICTOR TO ORAND, OVER and the reply ORAND TO PINTO V-VICTOR giving the QFE (the local barometric pressure) and permission to land. At this juncture I could almost hear and sniff the bacon and eggs frying. The night's work was nearly over. Our 24th operation almost safely completed.

We tumbled out of bed that day in time for lunch and, with this consumed, I played a few games of table tennis with Ray. If not good for one's digestion, it certainly kept one's reactions sharp. Half expecting another call to duty we sauntered back to our Nissen hut. Joe was there. 'Oi!' says he, 'we've finished our tour.' We laughed and turned away. But, stone the crows . . . It was correct! We were required to make up our log books and append two summaries. One, giving the day and night flying hours for June 1943 and the other giving the same detail for our spell of duty with 12 Squadron since February 1943.

Maurice came into the hut and we checked the news with him, then almost unbelievingly made out our log books as required and submitted them to the squadron leader's office. They were returned quickly and, sure enough, Squadron Leader Heywood had signed the June Summary and Wing Commander Woods had signed the squadron summary, to which he added in red ink: FIRST OPERATIONAL TOUR COMPLETED – 24 SORTIES.

To say that we were astonished and mystified is an understatement. How could this be? In the service generally one does not expect to get away with anything in the line of duty – in fact it is usually the reverse, duties are piled on. Thirty operations was the acknowledged standard length of tour and here we were with a deficit of six trips, (four in the skipper's case), yet, at least for the time being, that was all that was required of us. We were not disposed to argue the point but speculation was rife. No official reason was given but it may have been that new crews were passing through the OTUs in greater numbers and that the training units were short of instructors. Maurice was as much in the dark as the rest of us but, years later in correspondence, he ventured to suggest that we did our tour during one of the toughest periods for Bomber Command when 'Butch' Harris was experimenting with us for his theories. Also, all of our raids, except Spezia, were over Germany whereas, later on, the majority of raids were over France or coastal ports. It was then that a points system was introduced as the risk was much lower.* In addition, we had a fairly concentrated period of active service with not too many nights between raids and perhaps those in authority considered it better not to stretch our nerves any further – but who knows?

The tour had done my flying hours a lot of good. Daylight hours had only increased from 30 to 60 (!) but night flying had jumped from less than 5 to 146. About half of the latter figure must have been spent on trips to the Happy Valley, the balance being spent on targets elsewhere which I think is interesting for reasons I will attempt to explain. During the period of operations we were not aware that the Battle of the Ruhr, as such, was being fought. This only becomes obvious in retrospect. We were, of course, aware of taking part in something special, and generally, the ever-increasing success of raids was bound to have some impact on the progress of the war. However, our action was not confined only to the Ruhr. Indeed, for tactical reasons, Bomber Command could not concentrate solely on one area. To have done so would inevitably have invited the enemy to concentrate his defences at that spot which would have been counter-productive. An analysis of our tour appears to indicate how Bomber Command aimed to keep the German defence forces spread out. Taking the Ruhr area as a focal point we had visited Kiel in the northwest corner of Germany; Stettin far down the Baltic Sea; Berlin in the east of Germany; Munich deep in Bavaria and Stuttgart in the southwest corner near the French border. Was it planned that way or was it just random coincidence? My guess is the former.

At the end of the four-month period of the Battle of the Ruhr, Bomber Command could justly claim to have come out on top. Certainly, for the time being anyway, the Ruhr would not need a great deal of attention and, as matters turned out, very few additional raids were made in that area during the rest of 1943.

Out of the seventeen raids on the Ruhr in which we had taken part, a number were unsuccessful due mainly to adverse weather conditions or Pathfinder ground-marking difficulties. But certainly

---

* Harry, whose second tour covered this period, might not agree with this comment.

THE (UN)HAPPY VALLEY

OPERATIONS
March to June 1943

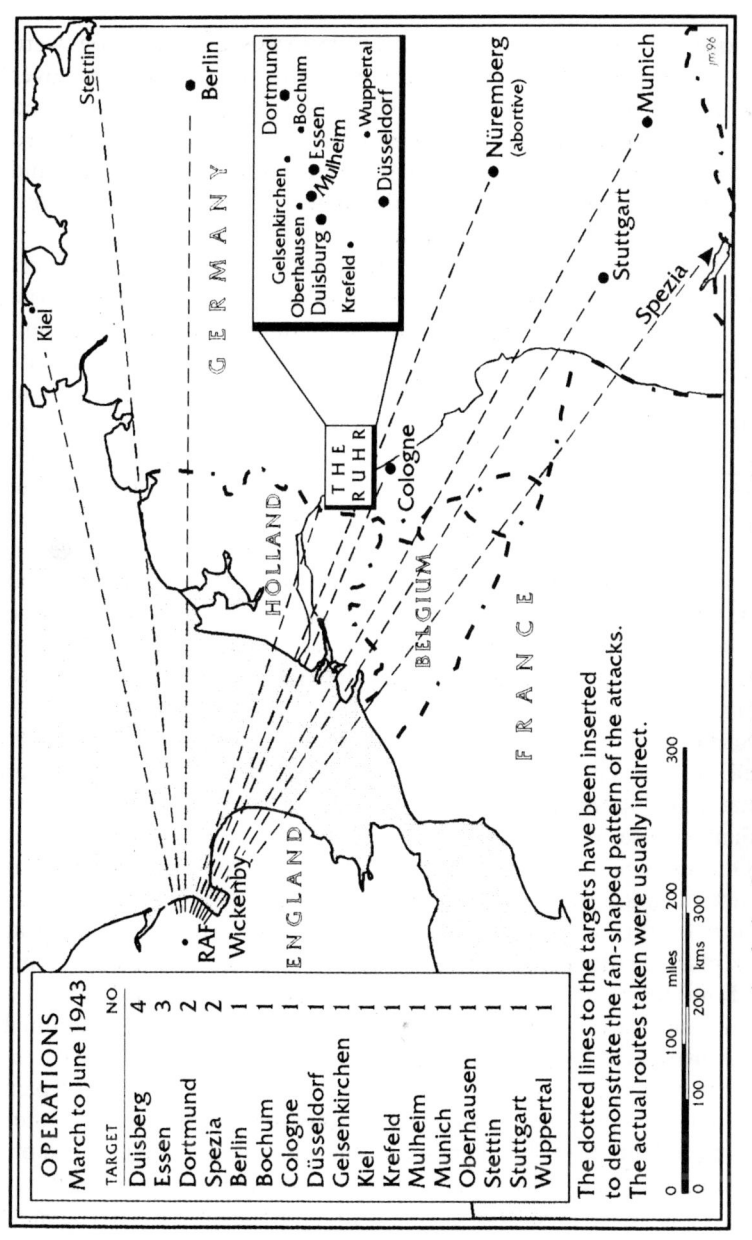

TARGET	NO
Duisberg	4
Essen	3
Dortmund	2
Spezia	2
Berlin	1
Bochum	1
Cologne	1
Düsseldorf	1
Gelsenkirchen	1
Kiel	1
Krefeld	1
Mulheim	1
Munich	1
Oberhausen	1
Stettin	1
Stuttgart	1
Wuppertal	1

The dotted lines to the targets have been inserted to demonstrate the fan-shaped pattern of the attacks. The actual routes taken were usually indirect.

Analysis of operations which demonstrates the wide raging variation of target choice

123

Oberhausen, Krefeld, Mulheim, and Wuppertal had all received mortal blows; Duisburg and Dortmund had suffered severe damage and Essen (particularly Krupps) had received substantial damage. Bochum too knew that we had visited them but, in addition, it was severely damaged along with Düsseldorf at a time when we were on leave. Further, the Dambusters' raid, apart from disrupting industry and causing damage, must have lowered the morale of the population. All the evidence points to the fact that heavy punishment had been inflicted during March to June 1943 and the weals from these lashings must have been felt deeply. Did the German population realise that the tide of war was turning against them? I don't know but for sure, although D-Day was still nearly a year away, we knew it was only a matter of time before Germany was totally defeated.

It was unfortunate for the Germans that the geographical position of their huge armaments industry was situated at a point nearest the British airfields and that their defences, although exceedingly strong and well organised, were insufficient to keep Bomber Command at bay. I believe I am correct in saying that as the result of bombings, they were obliged to disperse much of their industries to less vulnerable locations (indeed the accuracy achieved latterly must have made this essential) but the resultant decentralisation must have created organisational and other problems . . .

So much for the Ruhr, what about the other targets we bombed? Well, we had given a good account of ourselves at Stettin, Berlin, Munich and Spezia. Poor Spezia, this Ligurian Sea port set in the sunny Italian Riviera. We missed the warships but 'got' the town.

Our tour had ended, but action continued. The Battle of Berlin commenced later in 1943, when the longer nights permitted time for attacks on this more distant target. Before that, two significant raids took place on Hamburg – just a month after we had finished our tour. On both these raids about 750 aircraft had taken part. 'Window' (thin aluminium-backed paper strips) had been used for the first time thus blanking out the German radar equipment. Bomber Command losses were reduced (albeit temporarily) to a minimum, at a stroke – 1.5 per cent and 2.5 per cent respectively. However, on the second raid because of the prevailing conditions, an area of two square miles of Hamburg became a vast raging inferno which, in turn, caused a firestorm – an immense inrush of air to replace the rising convectional currents. This 'storm' lasted for three hours, at the end of which 40,000 people were dead. Afterwards one million of the population fled from the city in fear of further raids.

I mention this particularly because it seems to be an answer to those who would dispose of atomic bombs willy-nilly. A wind of change has blown throughout the world and there is hope that stocks of these weapons will be reduced in an orderly manner, although it is too much to hope that they will ever be completely phased out. But would we be better off without them? I doubt it. It would lead to a race for more and better conventional armaments which in the end, as demonstrated above (even 50 odd years ago) could be devastating. The deterrent factor of atomic bombs has kept us free from world wars since 1945. I am all for an agreed scale-down of atomic weapons but not extinction. It would be too dangerous, I fear.

I have mentioned elsewhere how well everyone at RAF Wickenby worked under pressure. The maintenance crews were splendid. We had no grumbles about their work. We experienced no engine failures or other troubles with aircraft equipment after our regretfully aborted first operation. No waiting about while final adjustments were being made. No bodging. They had a lot of pride in their work and their kite. Its welfare was their sole concern. Really, this was only a sample of the spirit which existed throughout the country. When people are united in a common cause, the sky's the limit. On looking back to those days in 1943, Tom, Dick and Harry, just ordinary chaps, drawn from all walks of life, had been trained to service these huge bombers which had been assembled by other teams of workers, some of whom may never have handled even a screwdriver pre-war. People found they were capable of doing work of a type they never thought they would be able to perform. The transition from peacetime to a war footing was achieved most successfully in an extraordinarily short time and the RAF was built up and expanded steadily and effectively. This was an enormous undertaking and the mind boggles as to how it was all planned and controlled. Hard work and application were the two essential ingredients but a large part of it was due to the spirit of the population and the will to succeed in the war.

Our crew awaited posting. We had come through a lot together and we were sorry to have to split up as a group but, obviously, we had no control or say over our future. The night before our postings became effective, we repaired to a pub in Lincoln – the only time the crew as a body had so assembled – we drank to each other's successful future and to V-VICTOR our Lanc which had served us so well. What happened to her (V-VICTOR a her? That can't be right!) Well, we must have passed our luck through to our successors. She survived the war having been transferred from 12 Squadron to 626 Squadron, then to 1 Lancaster Finishing School and on to 1656 Conversion Unit. Finally she was transferred to a Maintenance Unit and scrapped in July 1947. Of the other Lancasters we had flown on operations, Z crashed at Carnaby (an emergency strip); U was lost over Bochum; W and S were both lost over Holland and T over Mannheim.

No one had to be carried back to Wickenby. As I said at the beginning of this episode we were a very sober crew. The next day we exchanged addresses, bid each other the best of everything and departed.

SUMMARY FOR JUNE 1943

Date	Time	Aircraft	Pilot	Duty	Flying time	
14	22.55	Lancaster V	F/Sgt Wells	Operations	OBERHAUSEN	4.15 hrs
16	22.50	" V	"	"	COLOGNE	4.30 "
21	23.35	" V	"	"	KREFELD	4.00 "
22	23.15	" V	"	"	MULHEIM	4.05 "
24	23.00	" V	"	"	WUPPERTAL	5.00 "
25	23.00	" V	"	"	GELSENKIRCHEN	4.40 "

Despite all good intentions, in war time conditions it is difficult to keep in touch with colleagues. However, after the war, in one way or another, I managed to ascertain that all had survived. How had they fared?

MAURICE. Pilot. After a spell of training others at a Conversion Unit and probably frightening the life out of them with low-flying escapades, Maurice had a spell of glider-towing operations before and after D-Day. Later, he joined a New Zealand Squadron with Lincoln bombers. He would have operated against Japan, had the war not ended in 1945. He now lives happily at home in New Zealand where his house, in a prime position – with its three-quarters acre garden – overlooks Christchurch. A retired civil engineer, he is married, has five children and 22 grandchildren. He grows lots of citrus fruits and vegetables and has built himself a holiday home on the west coast which is situated in 43 acres. He was awarded the Distinguished Flying Medal after our tour.

JOE. Navigator. Completed a second tour which included the infamous Nuremburg disaster. I visited him at his home in Darlington in 1946. He had married and resumed his appointment with the local authority. He was awarded the Distinguished Flying Medal.

HARRY. Flight Engineer. Completed a second tour. Promoted to Warrant Officer, he remained in the RAF on permanent appointment after the war. He married a WAAF and is now retired and lives in Mablethorpe, Lincolnshire.

TOMMY. Bomb Aimer. Did not complete a second tour but after the war went to college and eventually gained a medical degree. He emigrated to Canada, married and settled down in Prince Edward Island to do good work as a gynaecologist.

TREVOR. Wireless Operator. Was awarded the Distinguished Flying Cross after our tour. I was not able to discover if he completed a second tour but after the war he returned to Rhodesia and carried on life as a farmer. He died some 15 years ago.

RAY. Rear Gunner. As with Trevor, I was not able to discover his movements after leaving Wickenby. However, he did not return to Rhodesia but married and lived in Birmingham after the war. He died about 10 years ago.

Maurice, Harry, Tommy and I were able to meet and attend a reunion meeting of the Wickenby Register in 1989.

Chapter 14

A Rest Period

On completion of our tour I was posted to a place called Tilstock which was situated on Prees Heath near Whitchurch – of blessed memory – in Shropshire. I found that an A Flight Lancaster, for some reason or other, was due to fly there, so I was able to hitch a lift. Might as well do it in style, rather than having to haul a couple of kit-bags between railway stations on an exasperating cross-country train journey involving many changes.

I arrived at 81 Operational Training Unit in Tilstock on 1 July 1943. Normally, 'screens', as we were called, were given a rest period of six months or so between tours and this period would usually be spent training new crews at the OTU.

As expected on the first day, I was called to the gunnery leader's office for a little chat. The opening pleasantries were completed quickly and then he posed the only real question of substance by asking:

'Are you interested in lecture training?'
'Yes sir.'
'Good.'
End of little chat.

I had, in fact thought deeply about training pupils and how I could best adapt to it. I suppose that I was in a better position than many. I had only finished training myself less than five months previously and had carefully preserved all my notes. The theoretical side of gunnery was still fresh in my mind and I was confident of being able to put it over successfully, even if I did not agree with some of the gospel propounded. I was quite prepared to teach any of a wide variety of subjects.

It was not long before I found myself in front of a batch of air gunners, all brand new sergeants. Gad, how young they looked! The chaps I had trained with had all been chosen from serving personnel and the average age was probably around the 23 mark. Looking at this new entry with all of my 25 years behind me I felt ancient. Most seemed to be only 18 years old and seven years makes a lot of difference at that age. I remembered a remark made by my previous gunnery leader to the effect that RAF gunners were adjudged to be just a fraction slow in action and split seconds in this game could mean the difference between life and death. It looked to me, therefore, that there had been a deliberate policy change and that youngsters were now taken direct from entry on call-up. They were all keen and bright eyed, full of life and good humoured. At times I couldn't help wondering what was in store for each of them and how innocent and unconcerned they were about their future. I had little doubt that some of them had only a few months or perhaps weeks of life to live but doubtless a lucky few would survive to tell the tale. Come what may I would do my best to help them.

Training was not confined to the classroom. Air-firing practice and cine-gun exercises were necessary. Whitley aircraft were in use at Tilstock. These twin-engined bombers had been used along with Blenheim, Hampdens, Wellingtons and others operationally since the beginning of the war and had penetrated the depths of Germany. Even up to November 1942, Whitley bombers had been used to bomb Berlin but were eventually phased out and converted to Coastal Command and training purposes. They were slow, cumbersome objects which deserved their nickname of 'flying coffins'. Communications were difficult fore and aft. One had to crawl between two sets of petrol tanks. Their lack of speed was evident even on local flying at Tilstock. What they must have been like on operations with full petrol and bomb loads doesn't bear thinking about. I take my hat off to those who operated in them. To me, flying in a Whitley after a tour on Lancasters was like riding around in a Morris 8 after being used to a Bentley.

A REST PERIOD

Our first trip was a disaster. We should have been carrying out a cine-gun exercise but failed to contact the 'fighter'. For some inexplicable reason the navigator had no idea where he was and had resorted to map reading. Even this had gone wrong and it had been left to the pilot to solve the problem but he could not pinpoint our position either. I was in the astrodome at this time and he intended to pass the map to me but this is where the whole thing came unstuck. The side window had been left open and as he passed the map over his shoulder the edge of the sheet caught in the slipstream and the map was sucked out of the window... Woosh... now you see it, now you don't. Cripes, consternation. So there we were – lost. No means of finding our way back to base, so what to do? Shortly we passed over an RAF airfield and the pilot, after some soul-searching, decided that he would ask for permission to land. He received it and down we went. The airfield happened to be Lichfield. I am not sure how the pilot played this Laurel and Hardy situation after landing, but I assume he reported some mechanical malfunction which, he thought, should be checked or perhaps he was a little short of fuel. Whatever the case, we stayed there overnight and proceeded back to base the next day. Well, that's one way of navigating but I'm glad to say that I did not experience a repetition of this sort of catastrophe on any future training flight.

Since I was likely to remain at Tilstock for some months, I had been trying to find local accommodation for Chic and Bowie. In a roundabout way I heard of a lady in Prees who had a spare room and would be willing to look after us. I won't mention her name but she was a good soul. She welcomed us to her home and we were treated more like her own children. She was undoubtedly the boss in the home and certainly controlled all the finances but her husband, an agricultural worker, was also quite a character. Three or four nights a week at about 8 p.m. he would clear his throat, look at his wife and if she nodded he would stand up, hold out his hand and she would produce sixpence from her purse. He would then pop off to the local for a drink, a chat and a game of darts. They were a happy couple who had developed a bond of understanding. Neither of them was ambitious and they were content with their lot in life. We in turn were happy to be there. Our married life together had, so far, been composed of short spells but for the first time we could

131

look forward, hopefully, to some months of stability. The gunnery section was situated a couple of miles away from Prees but I managed to buy a bicycle (demand heavy – supply short). It was a lady's bike albeit, which had a distinctly Edwardian look about its design. It must have been thirty years old at least, but never mind, I was able to use it to shuttle back and forth including lunch time. So for once we were able to live and enjoy something nearer a normal married life.

The countryside around Prees was quite pleasant and we could go for longish walks around the country lanes and enjoy the few weeks of summer that remained. Bowie was now nearly two years old. She was confident and observant of things around her. She could manage little walks and when tired she would spend lots of time being carried on my shoulders. It was a fascinating place for the young. A world full of daisies, buttercups and clover; frogs, birds and butterflies; of cows, sheep and nanny goats. We could wander through meadows, sit by streams under the trees and watch bunny rabbits playing in the fields opposite. We even managed a ride on a hay cart after lovingly, though with a certain caution, patting Dobbin's nose. Always on the way home we had to negotiate our way carefully past a black bull, who commanded his strip of territory aggressively and roared his disapproval at anyone who dared to go near.

There was no cinema in Prees. No entertainment of any sort, but it didn't matter, we were happy just to be together as a small family group. Eggs were a little more plentiful in the country than would have been the case in Sunderland and fruit in the form of apples and plums more readily available. We picked blackberries (brambles to us, being Northerners) in the lanes and mushrooms on occasions. All in all, life was very sweet but it couldn't last. I was due to go on an Air Gunnery Instructors' course at RAF Manby near Louth, in Lincolnshire. This necessitated Chic and Bowie having to return to the north-east for a spell. Two of us had been detailed for this course. The other was a chap I shall call Eric. We all travelled up to Manchester together before parting company.

RAF Manby was a quite well appointed and established station of pre-war standard. Eric and I had been sent there to learn how to teach. The staff had nearly all been drawn from the scholastic world and were exceedingly adept in putting over their subject. They had produced a basic instructional plan which if adhered to, was a good aid for preparing talks and lectures. This, combined with lecture technique – also taught – made easier the job of presenting a subject and imparting information successfully. Naturally, there is a limit to the amount of assistance the course could give. Good teachers are born, not made. Sheer knowledge on its own is not enough. I recollect that at my old school some of the best qualified teachers – holding PhD degrees – were not always good at putting over the spoken word in a simple, interesting and digestible form... It needed something more than being an expert on a subject. However, be that as it may, I found the course very helpful for the immediate task ahead, but further, I used some of the techniques I learned at Manby throughout my working life after the war, when situations demanded the speedy retraining of staff.

RAF Manby was situated in American Air Force country and on many days we were able to watch huge wings of the AAF Flying Fortresses forming and setting course for the continent. We were cheered to see their effort and in a bond of common sympathy silently wished them luck. Operating by night was one thing – daylight attacks were quite another. In locations where groups of British and American airmen met sometimes, the more misguided elements would start singing to the tune of John Brown's body:

> Flying Flying Fortresses at forty thousand feet,
> Flying Flying Fortresses at forty thousand feet,
> Flying Flying Fortresses at forty thousand feet,
> With bags of ammunition and a TEENY-WEENY BOMB.

followed by

> Flying Avro Lancasters at twenty thousand feet,
> Flying Avro Lancasters at twenty thousand feet,
> Flying Avro Lancasters at twenty thousand feet,
> with — ammunition and a GREAT BIG BOMB.

It always caused most unnecessary trouble especially if alcohol had been flowing for some hours. It is sad to reflect that group behaviour happens in many walks of life: in religion, politics, unions and trade associations. Groups sticking rigidly to their own parochial point of view are often abrasively intolerant of those holding opposite opinions. Man has much to learn about himself and his treatment of others – until he does, there is not much hope for care and understanding in the world.

The course was at an end. I travelled to Manchester where I had previously arranged to meet Chic. My small family arrived and in due course we boarded a train for Whitchurch. On the way, Chic asked what had happened to Eric. I told her that he was not returning to Tilstock and let her assume that he had been posted elsewhere. It was better not to mention that whilst at Manby we had taken part in a mock training exercise with local army units. Apparently in a fit of exuberance the pilot of the Blenheim in which Eric was flying had flown into a clump of trees. The aircraft exploded and scattered bits over a wide area. What a dreadful waste of young life. I never did really become used to the fact that during the war one's life was very tenuous indeed. It could be snuffed out so easily – just like a candle.

Back at Tilstock I resumed my routine but, since my six-months rest period was rapidly coming to an end and I was likely to be called for operational duty any day, Christmas was spent at Prees but we were able to travel to Sunderland for New Year. Near the end of this leave, a telegram arrived. A second tour posting? But no, I was required to report to the 93 Group Air Gunnery School at RAF Hixon. I was pleased about this posting in many ways but it caused immediate domestic problems. Chic's possessions and Bowie's gear were at Prees. However, these problems were overcome and I was free to go on my way to RAF Hixon.

This RAF station was located near Stafford. The school there had been set up for screened air gunners in the 93 Group of OTUs with the object of providing a refresher course and helping them to approach the problem of how to teach their pupils. A flight lieutenant was in charge of the school and the staff comprised a flying officer, a warrant officer and myself, now a newly promoted flight sergeant. I did not hold this rank for long, however, since I was to be commissioned and shortly afterwards I was appointed as a rookie pilot officer. It was early in 1944 and I was to commence one of the most interesting and satisfying jobs of my service life. In the following months, I was able to develop better ways of putting over the subject matter to those attending the fortnightly course. I really did enjoy the instructional training sessions and used to feel elated, when I found in examination answers that my own words were being repeated verbatim, indicating that I had sold the product successfully.

It was at Hixon that I first met a character named Sid Clewer, another pilot officer who had been posted in as a replacement. He was a practical joker who possessed a lively sense of humour. He could find fun in almost any situation. I have admittedly, a rather large nose. Amongst many references to this fact, two of Sid's quips stuck in my mind: 'Hey Doug, when you turned your head in the turret did your skipper have to apply the opposite rudder?' and 'No wonder you were coned by searchlights three times on ops – the Germans were curious about that strange shape in the sky!' At the time I did not know just how our lives would become interlinked.

Later that year the whole school was transferred to RAF Wymeswold near Loughborough and the powers that be decided that I should attend a Gunnery Leader's course at RAF Catfoss, situated near Beverley in Yorkshire. A short time before I was due to go, I was awakened early one June morning by the roar of many aircraft flying overhead. I jumped out of bed opened the door and looked upwards. The sky seemed full of Dakotas towing a couple of gliders apiece and flying somewhat west of south. Something was on obviously and, a little later, on the radio in the mess I heard Howard Marshall giving an on-the-spot description of the D-Day landings. His calm tones were full of confidence and assurance. The second front had opened. The day we had been looking forward to for so long was here. This was the beginning of the end. Being on a training unit, I had no prior warning of events and the whole thing had come as a surprise – but nevertheless I was pleased it had come. Had I been operating at that period I might, perhaps, have seen some of the action, since it seems that the entire Bomber Command force was engaged from 6 June onwards in direct bombing of German troop/gun positions and rail/road communications, plus ammunitions and oil dumps etc. This was a milestone in British history and I had missed it. I felt like the little boy that Santa Claus forgot.

I arrived at the Central Gunnery School at RAF Catfoss near the end of June 1944. A course at this establishment was the ultimate

Sid having a joke at the size of my nose – his was retroussé

Sid again – the extra hand points to his wound stripe, a favourite topic for line shooting.

goal of all air gunners since CGS was regarded as the authority which held dominion over all others. It was a tough course. All aspects of the trade were pursued to the bitter end and followed by a written test – very probing – which I passed successfully. In the air we did very little practical gunnery but day after day, for a whole month, we flew in Wellingtons on cine-gun exercises literally shooting off hundreds of feet of film at varied mock fighter attacks, which later could be assessed. This culminated in full-scale combat manoeuvres in which one gave a running commentary on the progress of an attacking fighter, preparing the pilot for the type of evasive action to be employed and giving the word 'go' at the critical moment for action. Interesting stuff this which supported the theory that gunners did not require guns or a gunsight but only the ability to judge the distance of an attacker, to anticipate the exact moment of attack (ie the point at which the attacker would open fire) and to be capable of advising the pilot just when and which manoeuvre was required to make the attacker miss and break away. Fighter attacks could be made at any angle (above, below, ahead or astern) and each type of approach had a counter-manoeuvre but the most common type of attack was known as the 'curve of pursuit'. In this case a fighter would usually first be seen on the port or starboard quarter. He would then pursue and attempt to come in on a line astern. If the attacker could do this he would be able to fire at point-blank range. The object therefore was to turn into his attack just before this vital stage was reached and, unless the fighter could turn inside the new line and lay off enough deflection, his shots would pass behind the bomber and he would be forced to break away.

All this was useful for daylight action but much reduced in value for Bomber Command crews, who were concerned with night raids only at this stage of the war. I would guess that in the case of the majority of crews shot down by fighters during the war their gunners never saw the attacker or, if they did, had insufficient time to give warning to take evasive action.

At Central Gunnery School much emphasis was placed on qualities of leadership. There are in life always people who are born leaders. Those who possess a good personality or appeal and have an immediate, sometimes compelling, influence on others around them. When this type of person also possesses the many other qualities such as knowledge, resourcefulness, tenacity, fitness, application, ability to organise and direct and so on, then one has a first class individual and obviously such people are in the minority. Personally, I did not see anyone on the course who was sufficiently outstanding to measure up to the standard set and this goes for myself too. Therefore how the staff arrived at their assessments I do not know.

After the course I returned to Wymeswold and resumed my teaching duties. Two months passed and then rumours started to fly that the whole of 93 Group was to close down and training would cease by the end of October 1944. The rumour turned out to be correct. Obviously our masters must have judged that the end of the war with Germany was reasonably within sight and the number of trained bomber crews was now to be reduced. So, shortly our school would close and we would be posted to other duties.

At the end of October Sid and I passed our probationary periods and had both been promoted to flying officer. The postings did not take long to take effect. We were to report to 1663 Conversion Unit at RAF Rufforth near York, where we would be crewed up for a second tour. Sid had been a rear gunner and I a mid-upper. Since we made a team we agreed to try and crew up together. We arrived at our new station and after the usual preliminaries we were eventually directed to a large room which contained aircrew of all descriptions. We were required to circulate and by common consent form ourselves into crews. How does one tackle this type of situation? How can one judge the qualities of people correctly at a glance and accept or reject almost on sight? We do discriminate in life day by day, often for very flimsy reasons, but usually it matters little whether we decide to like or dislike, trust or mistrust someone. Crewing up is different. One's neck is at risk. The job was made easier by the fact that neither Sid nor I wished to join a rookie crew and we quickly arrived at a conclusion (rightly or wrongly) that possibly this ruled out many of the chaps in the room. Of those left we spotted a flight lieutenant pilot at the bottom end of the room and made our approach.

'Want a couple of gunners?' we inquired (we must have sounded like a couple of spivs flogging kippers) and in a flash the deal was clinched. He had already gathered around him a navigator, bomb aimer and wireless operator – all second-tour flying officers. We had no doubts. We could hardly do better than this for, although the new skipper had not actually been on ops, he was a very experienced pilot. Now we only needed a flight engineer and shortly one was allocated. So, there we were, for better or for worse the marriage had been made. The die was cast. Between us we had decided our fate. The crew would comprise:

F/Lt 'RED' MORGAN. Pilot. Somewhat older than the rest of the crew. Probably aged 33. Had stacks of flying experience on training and graduation gun/searchlight duties. Had been a professional cartoonist pre-war. He was from Bristol. Quick, witty and ginger-haired, hence his nickname – nothing to do with politics, although he had a slight lean to port.
F/O FRANK BROWNE. Navigator. Born in the West Indies and spent his childhood there, but had lived in this country for some years. Small and thin, he had been employed by a local authority in the London area.
F/O TONY HEYWOOD. Bomb Aimer. A big chap from the West Country. Good personality and a dry sense of humour.
F/O 'WINDY' GALE. Wireless Operator. A professional golfer by trade. A friendly chap who could always be relied on to keep us in touch with the world over the intercom.
SGT EDDY —. Flight Engineer. I can't for the life of me remember his surname. He came from Hull and was a bright youngster who, as one might expect, had had experience as a motor mechanic.

Sid and I were well satisfied that we had made the right choice and hoped that the feeling was mutual. Unusually, four members of a crew were married but perhaps this was due to the average age being much higher than Maurice and Co. It was not long until I discovered that the wireless operator's wife Betty was expecting a baby and coincidentally, so was Chic. Our second was on the way. Since the children were to be born about the same time a bond developed between Betty and my wife and much correspondence ensued.

This time we would be flying in Halifaxes. At first we were not very pleased. Nothing could come up to the performance of Lancasters – the ship a sailor has just left is always the best – but in due course we warmed to them. The newer marks were faster and could fly higher (though not as high as Lancs) and certainly now had a better reputation. One feature we liked was that they appeared to be more substantially built than Lancasters, especially the massive undercarriage. Halifaxes were fitted with electrically operated gun turrets of the type I had used on Defiants. The only disadvantage was that the controls were not so easy to operate as those on the Frazer Nash turrets but one adjusted to this in time.

So, it was back to circuits and bumps – up, round and down; up, round and down *ad infinitum* it seemed, while Red, who had not flown four-engined craft, previously, gained experience. After hours we reached the stage of flying cross-country exercises which were more interesting. Other than Red, none of the crew had any experience of actually handling an aircraft in flight. It was advisable for at least one other member to have some knowledge of the controls and who would have some chance of taking over in an emergency – and who did Red nominate for this job – me! Ye Gods, I thought, he's crackers. Yet, of course, I was flattered. On the second cross-country run we were somewhere in the region of the Isle of Man, when Red called me to the cockpit. The kite was flying on automatic pilot (George), he vacated his seat and motioned me to take over. George was disengaged and the plane was all mine. My big moment had come. Probably the rest of the crew thought it was their last moment. They didn't say anything – perhaps they were using the time left in silent prayer. I found it all very difficult – I was surprised at first to find that reaction to control movement was very slow. I knew it would be, but I had expected something more positive. It took time to adjust to this and the tendency each time to overcorrect... but to keep the thing straight, level and on course all at the same time was problematical. To me, it seemed to be a long series of corrections and I never did really master the situation. We must have wallowed all over the sky, since there were yelps from the navigator from time to time leading to downright abuse about our erratic progress.

After twenty minutes or so Red nodded and grinned – the training session was over much to everyone's relief. There were a number of instances during the war of crew members having to take over the controls and even successfully landing aircraft. After my feeble efforts I admire their prowess. In theory I knew how to land a plane, but whether I could have accomplished this, without mishap, I doubt. The risks would be very high. Most chaps attempting this would need a lot of luck, but in my case it would have needed a miracle. Fortunately, it was never put to the test, but I would have had a go had the necessity arisen. I did hear of a squadron leader who taught his flight engineer to 'land' on cloud tops which seemed a good idea and the link trainer (a ground-based simulator) was available for practice IF one could obtain permission.

On the ground Sid and I, despite our background of instructional experience, had to go through the basics again along with the rookie gunners. We didn't mind really, one can always learn something, but a lot of it was precisely the stuff we had been putting over even before joining the Group Gunnery School. We coasted through and received our pay just the same.

As our course at RAF Rufforth progressed we carried out a 'bullseye' on London. A mock raid in which we played games with the searchlight defences as mentioned elsewhere. One evening three days later we were sitting in the mess when suddenly the staccato noise of exploding ammunition came to our ears. We all knew that could only mean one thing and going outside the mess a glow in the sky confirmed the fear that someone had crashed on the end of the main runway – another total write-off.

Two days later a Halifax was returning from a nickel (leaflet) raid. The base was fogbound but the pilot said he could see the runway lights and there was no need to divert elsewhere. In this situation the pilot has discretion and he was given permission to land. It was thought, however, that the pilot had mistaken the red lights at the end of a hangar for the red Drem-system lights on the runway and had made for them. He must have discovered his error too late and had not been able to overshoot. He crashed into the hangar and all the crew members were killed.

Everyone knew that crashes don't happen singly or in pairs – they usually happen in batches of three. Who would be next? The grim reaper had someone's name on his scythe.

The next night we were due to do our second last cross-country flight. It was quite a long trip of well over five hours but at last the lights of York came into view (the blackout restrictions had been lifted a little at this juncture). We were flying at 2,000 feet and Red was about to ask for permission to land, when suddenly there was an unearthly noise from somewhere. It sounded just like a tube train rushing at speed through an underground station. The constant speed unit on the port outer engine had failed and it was over-revving up to 4,000 r.p.m. The engine caught fire; the fire extinguishers failed to smother the flames which continued to spurt rearwards. We were almost over the base and Red promptly requested emergency landing. This granted, he hastily made his approach, simultaneously giving the order 'crash positions'. I scrambled out of my turret and opened the escape hatch over the wings just forward of the mid-upper turret. I sat down with my back against the rear of the rest bay and braced my feet against an upright projection – the laid-down drill. With arms folded across head in prescribed manner for protection, I was as safe as in any position in the aircraft. The engine was still on fire and milling at high speed but, with flaps and undercarriage down, we turned into the approach to the runway and the descent was under control. All seemed well... 400 feet up... 300 feet... then 200... down... down... steady... suddenly the port outer engine seized... Red couldn't hold the plane... She slewed to port, one wing low... carved a way through the tops of trees and hit an earth-banked Nissen hut, ripping out two engines and writing off the port undercarriage... The tail end, with Sid in the rear turret swung round through 180 degrees and demolished another ammunition filled hut... WE LANDED IN THE BOMB DUMP!

In my crash position I had not seen all these events, but as we hit the ground the H2S (radar) cover below shattered, the electrical equipment cascaded sparks and, with a horrible rasping sound, we ground to a halt. I remember thinking, somewhat unnecessarily – cor we've crashed – and immediately climbed up the wire ladder above and through the hatch in a twinkling. The whole kite was ablaze; its back had been broken. I jumped on to the wing which was greasy and slid down over the trailing edge and dropped ten feet to the ground. I knew that Sid would have turned his turret on to the beam (thus exposing the doors to the outside for escape purposes) and ran to the rear to see what had happened. I found him lying face down on the ground with his leg trapped between the turret and the back-end of the fuselage. His foot had been twisted round and pointed upwards. Somehow, with a mighty heave I managed to wrench his leg free and turn him over. He was slowly regaining consciousness and I pushed his head between his knees. Just then Red appeared followed shortly by Tony, Eddy and Frank; but where was Windy? In the light of the blazing aircraft we searched swiftly. After jumping from the plane he had sprinted away – a common occurrence after crashes – but had quickly become ensnared in barbed wire. We came across him trying to disentangle himself from his temporary incarceration and gave him a helping hand. Meanwhile, the fire engine had arrived with the ambulance. The fire was contained and prevented from spreading to other buildings by foam. Sid had been placed on a stretcher and we all followed him into the 'blood wagon' to be taken off to sick quarters. Except for a few scratches we were all OK, but obviously in a mild state of shock since we laughed uproariously at almost anything. Sid was detained in sick bay under observation but the rest of us were discharged and were taken back to the mess. No one could sleep. We sat in the mess until dawn broke talking over and over again about the details of the night's events. We now knew, to our cost, who was the third crew to crash in the current sequence – but – the grim reaper must have felt very annoyed with himself . . . He had taken a swipe – and missed.

We still had to complete our final cross-country flight in order to be regarded as a fully fledged crew and ready for operational duties. Sid had (probably unwisely, we thought) discharged himself from the sick bay and although very shaken, bruised and limping, claimed that he was fit for duty. It was five days later when we were detailed to fly again. Five days in which to cogitate about our near disaster. It was dark at dispersal and we stood outside this huge black forbidding monster apprehensively. None wished to fly; our confidence had been shaken. Red demonstrated true leadership by moving forward and exclaiming, 'Well, why are you all waiting?' Slowly we followed him 'creeping like snails unwillingly' . . .

Once in the air we felt better and all our troubles were forgotten – at least temporarily. We were somewhere south of Birmingham on our way back to base when the port outer engine (it just had to be) back-fired. Its performance became irregular with intermittent surges of power each time jerking the plane to starboard on its axis. No one spoke and we continued on our way like a crab with the twitch.

We were more than 30 minutes' flying time from base and were pleased when shortly Red asked for our opinion on what to do. There was unanimity – we wanted to land and have the aircraft serviced which, in retrospect, indicated just how low our morale had become. However, we were near RAF Wellesbourne and, with the port engine feathered, the skipper, having received permission, made an extremely good landing on three engines. We stayed at Wellesbourne overnight then proceeded back to base the next day without further trouble.

A surprise awaited us on return. We had expected to be posted to a Bomber Command squadron for operational duties but it just shows how wrong we were to assume anything of the sort. Instead, we were detailed to become part of a new 'special duty' flight which was being formed. We were intrigued, what sort of special duty would this be and where would it be performed? But this was not divulged. All that we could gather was that we would be located overseas. So, we were given four weeks' embarkation leave and sent home to await further instructions.

It was mid-December 1944 and one good thing was that Christmas would be spent at home. This really was a bonus. Whilst on leave I was required to receive inoculations at Fenham Barracks, Newcastle-on-Tyne and in London, of a type which indicated that a hot country was involved. The betting was that it would be India but only time

Chop, chop – the grim reaper ... had taken a swipe and missed

would tell. My leave was marred by one thing. I had not been able to throw-off the after-effects of our crash. I couldn't talk about it to my parents at home without making their problems greater. Chic was then four months pregnant and in the circumstances I did not wish to worry her with my mental stress. I was trying to repress my emotions and it wasn't doing me any good. I wanted to scream. I probably would have felt better had I been able to do so. Fortunately, my leave was extended and as time went by I became less strained and more like my usual ebullient self.

It was early February before instructions were received to report to RAF Melton Mowbray. The time had come to part once again from my wife and little daughter and step out into the unknown. Chic did not accompany me to the railway station. We embraced in the doorway and with a cheery chin-chin and a pat on the back I was off down the path to a waiting taxi. I looked back through the hedge. Chic was leaning against the doorway obviously very distressed. Would this be the last parting of the war? I fervently hoped so – five years plus of this type of uncertain existence was enough. I longed for the day when it would end.

The crew assembled at Melton Mowbray. All were in good form although Sid had suffered with boils during his leave presumably as an aftermath of the knocking about he had in the crash. However, perhaps now all of our questions about the future would be answered. They were – the new flight being formed would be known as 1341 (Special Duty) Flight. Red had been appointed as flight commander and the rest of the crew (excluding Eddy) would fill the section leaders' posts. In all, seven complete crews would form the flight. The other six crews had been selected at Rufforth and were all first tour chaps. Obviously this laid quite a responsibility on our shoulders. It seemed that we would have to lead from the front.

Next day we saw our new aircraft for the first time. They were Halifax IIIs in pristine condition and the clue to the special duties lay in the 'rest bay' of each aircraft. The seats had been stripped out and in their place, on each side of the aircraft, rows of electronic equipment had been installed. We were to fly out to an airfield on the west coast of India and specialist operators who would join us there, would use this equipment to pinpoint Japanese radar positions in the Burma area. So now we knew.

Flying trapeze at RAF Melton Mowby. Top L to R Eddy, Red, Doug. Bottom Sid, Windy, Frank

Chapter 15

A Second Tour

Before taking off for India some preliminary action was required. Early in March we flew to RAF Pershore. Here our Halifax was weighed and the following day a long 'consumption test' flight was made. All this I suppose was a necessary precursor before calculating what our range was likely to be and what fuel load we could carry prior to planning the long flight which lay ahead.

Having completed the preliminaries we took off for St Mawgan in Cornwall on 17 March 1945 and the following day at 08.15 precisely we were on the end of the runway ready for the beginning of our long journey, the first leg of which would take us over France via Poitiers, Toulouse and Sète, then over the Mediterranean Sea to Tripoli in Libya. We landed some nine hours later, at Castel Benito. In this short time we had been transposed into a different world. We had left the UK still virtually in winter conditions but now we were enjoying the warm North African sunshine, the palm trees, clean sandy beaches and the deep blue Mediterranean water. There was much evidence of the recent struggle between Monty and Rommel. Bits of aircraft and vehicles had been left strewn around; damaged and shell-scarred buildings abounded, some bearing hastily scrawled messages that booby traps had been detected, and so on. We walked into the desert a little way but decided that it was prudent not to wander too far. There could be mines or unexploded bomb-shells lying around. Beautiful anticylonic weather conditions prevailed. The air was so clear that it took time to adjust to judging distances especially at eventide. I remember standing hesitantly by the side of the road waiting to cross when an approaching vehicle was possibly 600 yards away and probably not doing more than 40 mph!

The food in the mess was superb – we had not tasted anything like it for so many years. If this was a fair sample of conditions overseas then, at least, we would be compensated to some extent. The service and facilities too, were better than at home but would this standard be maintained elsewhere? It was more than we dared hope.

After two days we were off to Cairo. Flying over the sea and desert alternately, we saw remains of ships and aircraft on or near the beaches and surprisingly, over the desert there was evidence of tank battles having taken place. I did not expect to see such since I thought desert storms would have obliterated all traces of tank tracks and that twisted bits of metal protruding from the sand or sand covered abandoned vehicles would be the only indication of where battles had taken place. But no – it was all there to see. Weather conditions must have been much more stable than one might suppose.

Cairo West Airport possessed a radio beacon. This made for easy navigation since we were able to home onto it. I was in the cockpit during our approach and had an excellent view of Cairo, the Nile Valley and Pyramids. In these days most of us are so used to travel abroad that we tend sometimes to be rather blasé and take things for granted; but in those far-off days the chances of seeing a scene of this description were negligible. I felt most privileged. We landed and as soon as the aircraft door was opened I realised that we were in for a hot time. It was hot. Or so we thought – we had no idea of what was to come.

Cairo was a pleasant enough city but even in the well-lit centre one had to watch out. Youngsters tended to roam around in mobs. Quite unprovoked they would choose an individual to push and jostle. Money, fountain pens and cigarette cases would disappear. It was better to leave such items at the mess/hotel but if items had to be carried then certainly not in an outside pocket. We learned quickly that it was no good shouting at these cheeky youngsters. This only succeeded in inviting greater annoyances. We gained the impression that British prestige was not high in Egypt despite the fact that the Eighth Army had saved their country from subjugation by the Germans. We stayed in Cairo for three days and saw the Museum, the Pyramids with the Sphynx and the Memphis Bazaar. We were very impressed with all of these attractions and the friendly and attentive Dragoman who conducted the tour.

We had a timetable to stick to and had to press on. The next stop would be Shaibah near Basra in Iraq. This RAF station was the subject of a well-known RAF song entitled 'The Shaibah Blues' so we were not expecting an idyllic haven. In pre-war days Shaibah had been regarded as a restricted-time station and this was an obvious pointer to the fact that conditions were not exactly congenial. However, we would be able to see for ourselves at first hand. The journey took us over the Suez Canal, the Sinai Peninsula, Palestine and Jordan – all the places of unrest since 1946. We picked up the oil pipe line and followed this eastwards (more or less) for 400 miles until turning for Shaibah. En route we wondered if we could or should visit Basra. After landing, we had no doubts. None, except Frank, wanted to do anything unnecessary. It was stifling, the mess was overcrowded, everything exuded heat and it was airless. The sort of place it was better to leave pronto. Although the conditions were undoubtedly bad and uncomfortable, part of our trouble was that we had not had nearly enough time to acclimatise.

Next day we were thankful to take off and reach the cooler air at 5,000 feet or so. We were bound for Karachi, a seven-hour trip over the Persian Gulf, the Gulf of Oman and then hugging the rugged mountainous sunbaked coast of Persia (Iran). Our stay at Karachi was brief and we proceeded quickly to New Delhi, then on to Allahabad to await events.

It seemed that the airfield we were ultimately to use was not available. Red had flown to South East Asia Command in Ceylon to find out what was happening but had received very little information. Meanwhile we waited, kicking our heels and wishing that someone, somewhere, would get a move on.

Each day seemed to be hotter. The mess at Phaphamau was very small and although it was equipped with fans, conditions were generally poor. An attempt had been made to keep the temperature down. The doors had a perforated zinc inset to allow air to enter and on the outside a coolie poured water down a rush curtain at regular intervals which, by evaporation, must have reduced the incoming air temperature a little. Since at the same time this increased the humidity I was very doubtful about its value. We had changed into lightweight khaki shorts and short-sleeved shirts but even these had drawbacks since if one's legs or forearms came into contact with the wooden chair frames, little bugs therein caused a nasty skin rash which remained for days. In the evening we could have been more comfortable by sitting outside on the verandah. But no, precautions had to be taken against mosquitoes and therefore long trousers and long shirt sleeves were to be worn. For good measure we should also have worn light calf length boots with which we were equipped to protect our ankles – but few did.

Sleeping was another problem in temperatures which rarely fell below 90 degrees all night. Had one been able to sprawl on a bed wearing something over one's tummy then I think sleep would have come more easily. However mosquito nets were provided and it was in one's best interest to use them. The mesh of the wretched things had to be very fine but the material also had to have sufficient depth to prevent a mosquito from inserting its proboscis through and helping itself to a measure of blood. The air inside the nets became stagnant which increased discomfiture but, in addition, pye dogs howled away at varying distances all night. Two or three hours of fitful sleep was about all that could be achieved. Most of the crew were feeling the heat as I was. The exception was Frank. Having been born in the West Indies where he spent his formative years, he seemed to take to the new conditions immediately. The hotter it was the better he liked it. This quiet introverted chap started to put on weight and became outgoing, genial, talkative and almost the life and soul of the party. The transition was hardly believable. The rest of us could have killed him but we didn't have the energy.

The next week conditions improved a little when we moved to the Royal Hotel in Allahabad. This establishment had been taken over by the RAF and was controlled by a catering officer. The rooms were larger, higher and more airy.

They contained much better furniture and the whole place was bright, polished and clean. The chap in charge had a breezy personality and insisted that we should sample a genuine Indian curry. We did. I quite enjoyed it but I have never touched the stuff since. Why?

Windy, Sid, Frank, Tomy, Eddy and Red outside the Royal Hotel, Allahahad

Well, the next day I suffered a dose of 'Delhi-belly'. So did most of the others. India was winning hands down. We did not go out of the hotel often. Indeed there was little to go out for. We had been dissuaded from eating in restaurants outside, especially things like salads and other uncooked foods. We were not allowed to have ice cubes in soft drinks and it seemed that anything that would make life more comfortable was taboo.

The streets around the hotel were dusty and one was subjected to blasts of hot air sometimes as the wind whipped up. These blasts of air felt as searing as opening an oven door when Yorkshire pudding is cooking. It drained one's energy. Dear reader, if you think we had an obsession about heat you are right – we had.

After a few days someone in authority decided that we should all be transferred to a transit camp and accordingly we were all posted to Poona. Our aircraft would be held at Allahabad and we would travel by train. That someone had a sense of humour. Poona must have been the best part of 1,000 train miles away. A lengthy journey by any standard. We wondered why we should be sent so far to the west when really we should have been going east. Had there been a change of policy perhaps? Could it be – and here wishful thinking entered the arena – that we were going to be repatriated. After all Poona was only 100 miles from Bombay. Not a chance, none would take a bet on that. We would just have to be patient. Despite the distance, the train journey turned out to be fairly comfortable and some of the scenery in the Narbada Valley between the Vindjya and Satpura Ranges of hills was quite attractive. The town of Poona was just the opposite in our opinion. We regarded it as an upholstered sewer and did not visit it again once settled at the transit camp.

Our accommodation was a sparsely furnished brick-built basha. Very basic, with a concrete floor, no ceiling and no plaster on the walls. Shutters covered the windows which had no glass. We wondered why. It did not take long to find out. Each afternoon at irregular intervals vicious little whirlwinds crossed the camp. They entered one side of the *basha* and left on the other. Anything loose on the table or elsewhere would be swept away, sometimes along with the exposed roof tiles. Ah well, this was something different and often quite airy. It did not take us long to organise against these intrusions and thereafter they just became part of everyday life.

Day after day we waited for our next move to be revealed but nothing happened. It was quite typical of service life as I have mentioned before – periods of deadly boredom followed by hectic activity. I had been used to the latter rather than the former which is just as well, since I like to be occupied doing things and making progress. We did have organised drill and exercises each morning but generally the rest of the day was free time. One afternoon I was taking photographs of some Indian labourers. One in particular interested me. His face had character unbefitting the ragged clothes he was wearing and he paused in his work whilst I took a shot. Red who was sitting close by saw the incident as a good subject for his artistic ability. In the twinkling of an eye, so the saying goes, he drew the scene of me looking somewhat superior taking the photograph of this unprivileged Indian but who, nevertheless, possessed a dignified composure. The caption was 'I take a dim view sahib' Very apt I thought.

Weeks went by, April turned to May and we were aware that the end of the war in Europe was near at hand – 8 May arrived and the signal that hostilities had ceased circulated quickly. This news was marvellous but the late afternoon timing was unfortunate. The beer and spirits immediately started to flow. Large wild and noisy parties were in progress all over the camp. Beds and tables were overturned, broken mugs, glasses and bottles strewn around; bods playing Tarzan and the apes on the roofs – and who was orderly officer that day... me! By 9 p.m. I could have had dozens in the guard room had it been big enough. By 10 p.m. every fire extinguisher had been activated – some in mock battles – foam was everywhere. It was useless to interfere. Had I done so, I would probably have been debagged and rest assured there would have been no witnesses. Eventually the whole *mêlée* subsided and in the early hours the camp became peaceful. It had to be; many were too drunk to do anything other than sleep where they were – in their clothes.

I had confined my activity to a watching brief and as far as possible ensuring that nobody injured themselves. The next day I expected to be hauled up in front of the CO to explain the shambles arising out of the night's activities but I wasn't. Obviously he understood.

Shortly after VE Day we were instructed to return to Allahabad – at last something was happening. After the long return train journey we arrived at RAF Phaphamau where we had left our Halifaxes and two days later we took off for RAF Digri which was situated about 50 miles north of Calcutta. This was to be our base.

We flew in. A fighter squadron was already stationed there and the airfield had been operational for some time. However our accommodation and the messes were separate and we saw very little of the other occupants.

From the air Digri appeared to be sunbaked and desolate but, in fact, the area was not devoid of vegetation. On the contrary, islands of trees and bushes were dotted around here and there, presumably as a check against soil erosion. Snakes were much in evidence locally and at night one had to be cautious of scorpions. We always carried torches. Lizards abounded everywhere outside and inside our sleeping quarters but we didn't mind, we regarded them as friends. Occasionally we would see a praying mantis. As we were in Bengal it was possible that tigers were around, but we didn't see or hear of any.

Our *bashas* were much better than those we had left behind at Poona and the mess was situated only thirty yards away. Not bad at all. Sid and I shared a *basha* and a young Indian was appointed as our batman. We never did find out his name but we called him George. He was a very willing fellow who kept our equipment and place clean and tidy. He fetched our tea, or whatever, when required but was a dreadful thief. Our cigarettes used to disappear in significant numbers but try as we may, we never did catch him doing it.

The sections had to be organised quickly. We knew that the monsoon would be upon us shortly. None of us knew what to expect but we thought that when it did break, our activities would be hindered. A snag arose since we were short of an armaments officer, which was a technical post. Normally I would have taken the gunnery leader's job but since I was willing to do the former I took over as such and Sid became gunnery leader. The two jobs anyway had close connections and we could and would liaise at will. Having talked to the other gunners generally it was evident that they were short of experience in fighter combat manoeuvres. Sid and I had a word with the local fighter boys and they were happy to come over and discuss what was required. After this we were able to carry out some useful practical fighter affiliation exercises.

Not long after we arrived at Digri, on entering the mess at lunch-time, I found myself confronted with a blackboard. On it was a drawing of my head in profile (my worst side, of course) above a baby's body complete with nappy and holding a cablegram. The caption was BOY OH BOY... The expected event had happened! I hastily opened the telegram and read: 'BABY BOY ARRIVED – BOTH DOING WELL.

Congratulations and back-slapping all round, of course, but the next 'all round' cost me a lot of money at the bar. Windy's baby had been born just a few days earlier, so the pair of us were now much pleased and relieved. Privately I was very sorry for Chic. Our two children had been born without me being present to give comfort and help. The first time I was 200 miles away as the crow flies but, at least, I would have leave in the foreseeable future. This time I was 6,000 miles away and no prospect of getting home until the war in the east ended. Life was hard – for both of us.

The heat continued to build up as June arrived although it did have one advantage, I remember. Each week an officer was appointed to dole out the pay. Each amount was not prepared in advance and placed in a packet as happens these days. Oh no, the amount to be paid was called out by the pay clerk. The recipient stepped up smartly, identified himself by calling the last three figures of his service number and the amount to be paid was counted out in front of him. The snag was that payment was made in paper money. There was little chance of underpaying someone but there was a risk of overpayment because of notes sticking together. However, at the end of the pay parade, having processed thousands of notes, the sum remaining was always exactly the balance required. The secret was that one's fingers were nearly always damp but in the event of them drying out a quick dab inside one's shirt found an ample reservoir of perspiration to supply the necessary moisture.

Flying was an uncomfortable experience at times. Planes exposed to the sun on the ground during the day frequently had an internal temperature in excess of 130°. We entered the aircraft clothed only in shirt and shorts. By the time the runway was reached our clothing would be wet through. At 5,000 feet and above in the turret or any part of the fuselage aft of the cockpit, the draught felt freezing and I was never able to overcome this discomfort problem satisfactorily. Sufficient to say perhaps that none of us appeared to suffer any health problem as a result of these sudden and drastic changes of temperature. On the ground we did our best to avoid the worst of the heat by rising early each morning and were usually in the office by 7 a.m. The idea was to do what was required during the morning, finish before 1 p.m., have lunch, and then retire to bed for a siesta. This was the only practical solution – it really was too hot for anything else. Two airmen had already died from heat stroke. Conditions were such that we could not afford to take any risks especially in our unacclimatised condition even after three months. We drank salty water twice a day on the advice of the medical officer who had counselled us that we should not, on any account, let ourselves become short of liquid. We had no choice really. Each hour of the day we drank something or other.

THE TURRETS OF WAR

Personnel and Halifax Bomber of 1341 (SD) flight at RAF Digri – August 1945

One afternoon at about 4.30 George came in carrying our tea. He set it down on the table and pointed to the window, muttering some unintelligible remark. We looked out and almost immediately the sky changed from blue to an orange hue, the wind suddenly whipped up and a sandstorm swept down the gap between the two sets of *bashas*. Conditions had changed from dead calm to a raging 60 m.p.h. storm in a couple of seconds. The sandstorm continued for five minutes and was immediately followed by hail turning to torrential rain which was accompanied by lightning and thunder the intensity of which was of the severest type experienced at home. This storm lasted for an hour then eased and rolled on its way in a north-westerly direction to flicker all night over the distant Himalayas. The monsoon had started. Each evening from now onwards at ever advancing times we would receive this treatment. One could almost set one's watch by it.

This was the first rain in the area for several months and was welcomed by the indigenous population. It was also welcomed by the bullfrogs which came out from nowhere in great numbers and croaked their way through the night. They were so irritating that one member of our mess, a golfer who shall remain nameless (not Windy I might add), used to go out each evening with a torch and a mashie-niblick and practise his skills in seeing how far he could drive their severed heads. He also applied similar treatment to the scorpions. As I look back on such actions which were very cruel, I am convinced that this individual would not have done anything like it at home. He was probably a little unbalanced by the conditions, as possibly we all were. On another occasion two other chaps went out in the evening to a wooden area to the rear of the mess – a rather dangerous thing to do anyway – it was nearly dark and there was some movement the bushes. One of them fired his revolver to ward off a possible attack by an animal. Later that evening a complaint was received by the RAF police that an Indian native had been fired at. Two sergeants were identified as being involved. Next morning the police held an inquiry – and who was the orderly officer who would have to attend the hearing? Me. I always seemed to catch out. This placed me in an invidious position since I had heard of the incident in the mess. Fortunately, the two sergeants had ample evidence to prove that they were in their hut at the time of the incident. They were therefore released without more a do. I was much relieved and, since no harm had actually occurred, no further action need be taken. Had we had a dead body on our hands it would have been a different matter.

The monsoon caused an increase in humidity. As a result most of us suffered from prickly heat. This malady was caused by perspiration breaking through the skin (due to overworked pores). A rash developed over most of the body but more especially on the chest and back. This made one irritable and there was no real treatment available. Bathing twice a day and application of calamine lotion relieved the condition a little but the only sure cure was to move to drier and cooler conditions. Because of this I was anxious to visit a hill station and eventually I managed to arrange a spell of leave in Darjeeling which lies about 6,000 feet up in the foothills of the Himalayan mountains.

I booked in at the Grand Hotel in Calcutta overnight. This well-known establishment must have been visited by a multitude of serving personnel during the war. Situated in Chowringee it seemed to be the centre of the world at the time. Outside, the pavements were lined with street traders who would sell anything from a candlestick to a lucky bean purse or a kukri to an ornamental box. One just had to haggle. Full of humour these crafty fellows were adept at bargaining and try as one may after purchasing an article one always had an unhappy feeling that the finally agreed price was too much. They probably made a small fortune out of British and other servicemen during the war, but it was good fun.

Calcutta teemed with humanity. It seemed to be overcrowded. Everywhere a mixture of Indian nationals (sic), Hindus, Moslems, Sikhs and Parsees. Some in native clothing, others in western dress and saried ladies all combined along with service uniforms of every type to make a colourful, kaleidoscopic scene. Overloaded trams with youngsters clinging dangerously to the sides rattled their way through crowds of rickshaws and tongas. The whole place buzzed. On the other hand sacred cows were left to roam the streets at will and beggars, some horrifically malformed, pleaded mournfully for baksheesh on almost every street corner.

The newspapers at that time were very critical of the British administration of their country. Each day brought fresh headlines alleging unfairness or mismanagement. The media were certainly whipping up anti-British feelings in the native population and causing resentment. Obviously independence for India could not be denied much longer. Personally I felt that we (the British) had developed their country very well considering all things. It had been built up and administered as at home. Everything required by a modern society was available – communications, utilities, law, medicine, education, commerce and so on – all seemed to be working smoothly. In addition along with their forces we had prevented a possible invasion of India by Japan. However, we were not wanted and the rest of the story is history.

Calcutta Railway Station had the same lively buzz about it as I caught the train to the base of the foothills, where a small-gauge railway equipped with powerful little engines chugged their way up the short but steep slopes to Darjeeling. The heat of India was soon left behind on the plains. What a relief to rise above them and into the cooler fresher mountain air! The vegetation changed with height and at 5,000 feet the scenery was fresh and green, the trees reminiscent of those at home. Life was already more comfortable. Another 1,000 feet and Darjeeling station appeared. This smallish town was well known as a centre for the tea trade. Situated on a hillside it looked attractive and seemed to be almost like the Lake District in character. It was really situated in Gurkha country since the borders of Nepal and Sikkim were close by. The residents were small and tough. I felt ashamed when a small seemingly old lady, less than five feet in height, placed my heavy case in a head-sling and made off at speed up the hill to the Mount Everest Hotel some distance away. I bashfully paid her a rupee for this service which was probably three times the going rate.

Monsoon clouds hung over the town and the valleys were misty, but the air was fresh and I enjoyed breathing in great dollops and blowing it out like a spouting whale. Nevertheless, I felt more like a convalescent invalid after a long illness, my back ached and I felt weak. I had not realised just what a toil the heat of India had taken. I had lost a stone in weight.

I hoped that, in a few days in this environment, I would revive. I did. Almost immediately the prickly heat disappeared and quickly my strength returned. My desire to see round the next corner and to explore the countryside on foot or horseback was back to normal.

The Mount Everest Hotel was first rate. It stood at one end of the town in a commanding position. It was well appointed and the food was marvellous. It must have been a haven pre-war for the privileged visitor but now it had been taken over for military use and abounded with British, Commonwealth and American types from all three services. The atmosphere was friendly. No fights or squabbles between the various factions. Everyone intended to enjoy their stay. Discussions about world conditions were a favourite subject for debate and nearly always the conclusion reached was that after the war there must be more co-operation between peoples, particularly those in the western world. On reflection I think that in the intervening years we have seen quite a movement in this direction. The Common Market is a good example while still retaining Commonwealth links and, of course, America has not, to date, pursued an isolationist policy. Quite the opposite in fact and the formation of NATO has helped.

The cloud remained low all week but one morning I was awakened by a bearer urging me to rise. Excitedly he was saying, 'Quickly sahib – Kanchenjunga can be seen, come outside.' I jumped out of bed and ran to the terrace – I gasped – there across the broad valley the massive mountain lay shimmering in the early morning sun. Only 72 kilometres distant, this 28,000–foot monster filled the width of the horizon. Newly clothed in its monsoon snows, Kanchenjunga reflected the sun's rays with such intensity that one could only gaze at it for very short periods. It remained visible for about an hour. The clouds slowly closed in to obliterate the scene and the mountain did not appear again during the time I was in Darjeeling. I was glad to have seen the world's second highest mountain. The top of Mount Everest can be seen from a point about six miles outside Darjeeling at a place called Tiger Hill but, according to the locals, at no time were conditions such that it was worth making the journey. A pity, since as a boy I had read avidly all the accounts of expeditions to date. I had also attended a lecture by Frank Smythe who had climbed the highest on Everest at that time and was therefore my boyhood hero.

Next day the unexpected happened. News spread rapidly that the Americans had dropped a super-powerful atomic bomb on Japan which had caused unprecedented damage and had threatened to drop another, if the Japanese did not cease hostilities immediately.

The rest of the story is history but what a relief! The end of the war had arrived unpredictably early and I could hardly believe it. It took time to adjust. That I could now think about the future with a degree of certainty was something I had not dared to do for so many years. It was a new and very comforting situation.

Although there were a few orgies, the peculiar thing was that the attitude of guests at the hotel was quite different to that on VE Day at Poona. The place was quite calm generally. The big question which now exercised the mind was how long would it take for demobilisation plans to be put into effect? A system of awarding points on an age-plus-length-of-service basis had been worked out which ensured that the older and longer-serving personnel would be released first. Having been in the RAF since day three of the war worked in my favour and, although I would not be amongst the earliest group for demob, I should not have too long to wait – perhaps three months or so.

My leave was at an end in Darjeeling and I chugged-chugged down the little railway in much better shape than on the upward journey. Back at base I found that I had been posted to Group Headquarters in New Delhi. I was rather pleased about this since it would give me the opportunity of seeing something of that famous city.

As soon as the war finished, activity generally decreased all round and my task at Group HQ, which concerned squadron strengths and serviceability, could be completed in about four hours. Every afternoon was therefore free. I was working in the centre of New Delhi only a hundred yards away from Government House. It was a pleasure to live and work in such surroundings. Not only that, as weeks went by the temperature fell and conditions by mid-October became similar to the best of British weather. We wore khaki shorts and shirts each day but at night it had become sufficiently cool to change into blue. At last I was living a normal life. Each afternoon was spent playing bridge and swimming in the pool belonging to the nearby Hotel Cecil which had been allocated to us. No prickly heat to contend with and no other skin troubles such as monsoon sores made life happier and I was developing a beautiful bronzed tan from the constant exposure to the sun each day. All this plus dinner in the evenings at Davico's restaurant in Connaught Place (the equivalent to Mayfair perhaps) made me feel I was living the life of a *borra sahib*. I had changed substantially from the miserable wretch I must have been only two months previously.

The group numbers for release were creeping up... 18... 19... 20 ticked by and I was looking for 25. Things started to move quickly and it seemed that I had hardly time to turn round when I was packing my bags and boarding the train for Bombay. I could have opted to go home by air. I was sorely tempted. After all the UK was only about 24 hours' total flying time away. Aircraft were plying to and fro in great numbers daily and it was known to be easy to hitch a lift. But no, discretion was the better part of valour. I had diced enough during the war and there was no point in tempting providence yet again. I would proceed by sea – a little longer but safer.

Bombay is known as the gateway of India. Well, all I wanted to do was to go through it the opposite way. A few days had to be wasted waiting for a ship and these were spent largely lazing in the sun at Breach Candy, a beautifully landscaped open-air swimming pool set in acres of ground. The hardest work here was to ensure that the hawks did not steal one's food. These nasty tattered creatures appear all over India. They are seekers of carrion but they never miss an opportunity if other types of food are available. I had always been able to prevent them from pinching any of my food but on my last day at Breach Candy I fell for the oldest trick in the book. I was eating a sandwich and warily watching a kitehawk – or something which sounds like it – hovering in front of me 30 feet up, when suddenly another came from behind and whoosh, my sandwich soared into the air. To lose one's sandwich was bad enough. To be beaten tactically by two of those rotten squawkers on the last day was unbearable. I wished for a turret and bags of ammunition but such was not available. Uselessly, I threw a stone at the offender. My pride was hurt.

Next day was the one we had all been waiting for. Hundreds of us flung our kit into the backs of open lorries and climbed aboard. The QETV *Queen of Bermuda* was waiting at the docks. The *Queen* as she was known had been used for pleasure cruising purposes in the Caribbean pre-war and was a luxury vessel. Ah well, why not go home in style? But it wasn't quite like that. Most of the luxurious fittings had been stripped out and she was now nothing more than a trooper.

Worse was to come. Two of the four turbines were not working and her speed was therefore reduced to 14 knots. This meant that the journey would take nearly three weeks to complete. The date was the 1 December 1945. We would have to keep our fingers crossed. If anything further went wrong we might not arrive home in time for Christmas.

Bombay was fading from sight as the turbine's full power was switched on. The boat didn't exactly leap out of the water but it would do, provided they kept going. The Arabian Sea was dead calm. The water was crystal clear and in the shadow of the ship we could see that we were being accompanied by many large (tunny?) fish. Flying fish, too, skimmed the water. RAF types were amazed. The naval chaps were amused that we should take such an interest in what to them was a mundane scene. Anyway we were doing nicely at about 300 miles a day and that's all that mattered. We passed Aden with its huge oil storage tanks shimmering in the sun then turned into the Red Sea and through the Suez Canal into the Mediterranean. We were approaching Sicily when another ship appeared over the horizon behind us. It was rapidly overtaking and by the looks of the huge single funnel it was probably the *Louis Pasteur*, which had left Bombay days after us. This 'crack' liner was the pride of France and capable of 30 knots. As it drew nearer there was no doubt as to its identity. It was the aforesaid. Lucky old Sid was on it and as it flashed by, I could almost hear his laughter after telling those around him, 'It's Doug's nose, you know, that's holding the *Queen* back.' But not to worry, despite a massive storm in the Bay we managed to dock in Liverpool on 19 December and two days later arrived home for Christmas.

Did I ever operate from RAF Digri? No. Only on operational trip was made and the operator thought that he had detected a Japanese radar station but on return it was decided that he had only 'fixed' on his own equipment. It had all been a waste of time and effort. As a second tour it was a washout . . . As a sightseeing tour it certainly had its moments. More like a Cook's Tour really. Later I heard that after helping with the repatriation of the prisoners of war programme, our Halifaxes had been scrapped in India. Still, that was better perhaps than losing them over Burma or other Japanese-held territory. Had the Big Bomb not been dropped it would have been necessary to fight all the way. It is anyone's guess how long this would have taken and how many millions of additional lives would have been lost. Despite the severe damage to Nagasaki and Hiroshima and the radiation problems that followed there was no argument about the correctness of using the atomic bomb. It saved a lot of bloodshed then and has done so since.

The last I heard of Sid he had settled down in Tetbury, Gloucestershire. His back was giving him trouble. I was not surprised considering the mauling he had sustained. I met Frank in Whitehall one day and again later in Gravesend, Kent. Red and Eddy stayed on in India, I believe, ferrying supplies over the 'hump' but of the others I know not.

I shed my uniform, on my first day home. The day I had been waiting for patiently, nay dreamed of, for more than six long years, had come – I could hardly believe it. Home with Chic, Bowie and now my little son, whom I could see and hold for the first time. I was a lucky man to have them. I was also one of those lucky enough to 'get away with it'. So many that I knew had paid the ultimate penalty. My photograph of the Wickenby Memorial is a constant reminder.

Chic and the family photographed in the heavy snows of early 1947

Afterthoughts

About fifteen years ago Chic and I were on holiday in Honolulu and we took the opportunity to visit the American Naval Base at Pearl Harbor which the Japanese, without warning, attacked from the air in 1941. We toured the harbour by boat and saw where many of their warships were sunk – now a little more than hunks of twisted, rusty metal protruding above water level. On approaching the site where the United States Ship *Arizona* lies, little could be seen, but a memorial to the crew of over one thousand who were killed when the ship exploded has been built exactly over, and in the shape of, the Arizona's bridge.

Our boat stopped at the memorial. The engines were switched off and a wreath was placed on the water. A minute's silence commenced. The moment was too much for many present and tears began to flow... emotions had surfaced and the pain of grief was evident on the faces of those around us... Doubtless, some had lost family members in the disaster but, perhaps to other Americans this spot signified the start of the Second World War and all the tragedies which ensued. Both Chic and I were affected by the scene. We fully empathised with them. We felt deeply that if ever the futility of war was totally demonstrated, it was here. There was little conversation on the return journey to Honolulu. Our thoughts were too full of the horrors of war and man's inhumanity to man.

I become irritated, sometimes, when I hear comments about war being made by people who have had no experience of hostilities. The commemoration of the two World Wars at the Cenotaph in London each year is sometimes described, cynically, as the 'glorification of war'. But, I am sure that those who march past the Cenotaph and have been in action would not consider that war is exalting in any way. It is a long, hard and dangerous struggle, carried out with grim determination. Let me give you an example.

In late April 1943 a Lancaster pilot, Laurie Lawrence, and his crew were detailed to lay mines in the sea off Gdynia, Poland. From 12 Squadron they were one of ten aircraft taking part. This operation was a tremendous undertaking since it is a long trip down the Baltic Sea and at that time of the year nights are becoming short. Unfortunately for Laurie, his own plane was found to be unserviceable and he, along with his crew, had to transfer to a reserve aircraft. This cannot be done quickly and when they arrived at the end of the runway for take-off vital time had been lost. Their operation should have been cancelled but, because a maximum effort had been promised, Laurie – against his better judgement – was persuaded to go. He did so, knowing full well that he had no chance of catching up with the main stream and would be on his own. A highly hazardous situation.

All went well on the outward journey apart from flak over Denmark and from Baltic Shore Batteries and the mines were laid as required. As they turned for home, they were not aware that already four of the original ten planes had crashed into the Baltic Sea or nearby, and all the crews had been killed. But, they had their own problems... It was impossible for them to reach the western coast of Denmark before dawn – the possibility of fighter interception was almost inevitable – and so it proved... Just off the coast, in half light, the rear gunner spotted a Ju 88 fighter curving in from slightly below on the port quarter. He yelled 'dive port', firing his guns simultaneously. Laurie immediately responded... too late... the Ju 88 had fired a long burst of cannon shells. The plane shuddered and dived steeply to port... all hell let loose... the rear gunner had been blinded – the mid-upper gunner had been blown out of his turret and was badly wounded in his leg... The aircraft was defenceless and the wireless operator could not reach the astrodome to watch for the Ju 88 because of the effects of G... Laurie, with the aid of his engineer and bomb aimer fought with the controls as they fell from 12,000 to 6,000 feet in a spiralling, accelerating horrendous dive and eventually managed to pull out and regain an even keel. One moment's relaxation and the aircraft again whipped over and dived to port. The struggle to regain control was repeated but they had plunged from 6,000 to 2,000 feet before the aircraft levelled out. At this point it was discovered that the port aileron had been blown away and that the aircraft could only be flown with full starboard control column and rudder. In addition an elevator had been damaged. Fortunately, as they pulled out they noticed cloud cover and happily nosed into it. The Ju 88 was not seen again – perhaps the rear gunner's burst of fire had struck home. Who can tell – suffice to say the attack was not renewed.

A decision had to be made as the aircraft could not turn to starboard and only the minutest turn could be made to port – albeit at the risk of another catastrophic dive which would probably plunge them into the sea. The gunners were very badly injured and suffering grievously until given some relief by injections of morphine... The aircraft was heading roughly in the direction of Mablethorpe and then had some 350 miles to go. As the plane gradually edged to port it was decided to attempt a landing at the nearest drome. It was estimated that they could make landfall in a little under two hours. Because the rudder bar had to be maintained fully to starboard it was not long before Laurie experienced cramp in his right leg. Ingeniously, Bert Cruse managed to arrange a metal bar between the base of the pilot's seat and the rudder pedal thus relieving the pressure on the skipper's leg. This made life a little easier although the bar had to be adjusted each time the course needed to be altered.

Eventually land was sighted, visibility was good and ahead the lights of RAF Coltishall could be seen. This drome had no runway – only grass – and this was a distinct advantage. Laurie was unaware of the exact damage to the aircraft and there was a distinct possibility that the hydraulic system had been damaged and that he would have to make a belly landing... He gave those of the crew, who could be spared, the option of descending by parachute but they refused. So, with the bomb aimer remaining in the nose helping to apply full starboard rudder and the engineer assisting with the control column they prepared to land but they were painfully aware that to prevent the aircraft from becoming unmanageable the landing would have to be made at above normal speed. Fortunately, the approach to Coltishall was from the starboard side and Laurie was able to make a very slow turn into wind. Eventually he lined up but his approach was erratic and with highly milling engines each adjustment as they slowly lost height made for nail-biting tension... down, down... steady – would the undercarriage work? If it did, would it upset the plane's equilibrium? The order was given for it to be lowered... they held their breaths... it worked! Laurie eased the craft on to the grass surface reflecting that a crosswind landing on a runway might have proved too tricky and ended with fatal results.

Wow... It makes my flesh creep even to think of it... The two gunners were taken to Norwich Hospital – they would never fly again. The rear gunner later on was repatriated to Canada and regained partial sight. The mid-upper gunner unfortunately had to have his right leg amputated. For his valiant efforts Laurie (Flight Sergeant Charles Oliver Alfred Lawrence) was awarded an immediate Distinguished Flying Medal.

A long story – war stories often are – but what can be deduced from the facts? So far as 12 Squadron were concerned, the operation had caused the loss of four Lancaster bombers (40 per cent) and the lives of 28 aircrew. In addition, a further Lancaster was so badly mauled, its write-off was a possibility, and two gunners so badly wounded that their discharge from the RAF was inevitable. A very heavy price to pay for a night's work. But what of Laurie and his crew? Two qualities stand out – skill and grim determination. If, at the time, I could have asked Laurie if he thought there was any glory in what he had accomplished, I am sure he would have shrugged and replied in the negative. After reflecting awhile he might have added quietly – the job was there to do and we did it. His main concern was the anxiety over the injuries to the two air gunners and their survival.

The battles fought by both Fighter Command and Bomber Command during the war were acclaimed by the public generally yet, after hostilities ceased, criticism of both commanders-in-chief, Lord Dowding and Sir Arthur Harris respectively, became the order of the day. All this, despite the fact that Fighter Command in the Battle of Britain (1940) undeniably saved the country, single handed, from invasion and that later Bomber Command's action greatly weakened the enemy's manpower and material resources, thus bringing war to a successful conclusion sooner than would otherwise have been possible. What, I wonder, was the reason for this paradox? Could it be that the press, bereft of war news was seeking sensational headlines elsewhere? Or the cries of left-wing politicians seeking to denigrate our war achievements and boost those of Russia? Or was it interdepartmental jealousies? In the post-war restructuring of the armed forces both the Navy and Army would need to fight hard to retain their strengths and equipment. Over the years I have seen many letters in the press suggesting that the Royal Air Force should not be a separate service but should be split between the Navy and the Army who would have complete control. This nearly happened pre-war. Fortunately, the proposal was rejected otherwise, for sure, we would never have had the capability, in the air, to defend and attack in the way it happened during the war. Nevertheless, the opinion in Navy and Army circles remains the same today. They don't seem to have learnt anything from recent history.

In some quarters, Bomber Command's actions were criticised because of area bombing which caused high civilian casualties and particularly the killing of old people and children in raids. Yes, but let's put the picture into perspective. Germany has been responsible for two World Wars this century. The First World war mainly concerned the armed forces, and civilians, apart from those in the battle zones, were not affected to any extent other than those killed or wounded by Zeppelin raids. The Second World War was quite different. Germany overran the major part of Europe, using air power at will, and following with ground strikes in order to gain a foothold and eventually subjugate the populations of many countries. Their régime was brutal, heartless and inhuman. For six years they caused misery to untold millions of people who were forced to submit and even help their conquerors, in fear of their lives. All civilians young and old alike were very much affected. After the fall of France it was the turn of London which was blitzed night after night over a long period. Many were obliged to sleep and even spend their lives in underground stations. Coventry and most large industrial towns received a pounding and, later on, London was again subjected to bombardment by V1 and V2 missiles and rockets. Civilian casualties were high up and down the country, and the public at home rightly expected that our reprisals, when they started, would be gruelling, as indeed they were.

Obviously the primary policy behind bombing must be to destroy industry – particularly that concerned with producing warlike stores and materials required for the armed forces. In industrial centres, factories and plants were surrounded by residential areas so it follows that the latter would always be in danger. It simply is not possible to bomb one without the other. Bomber Command did not have the sophisticated equipment which is currently in use (guided bombs etc). Targets were difficult to pinpoint at night. These were often obscured by industrial haze (especially in the Ruhr), fog, mist or by smokescreens. Sometimes targets were partially or wholly covered in cloud. In late 1940 raids on specific targets were attempted and precision-bombing techniques were tried. However, it was found that the outcome was ineffective and thought was needed to be given to the *modus operandi*.

It is an odd fact that the Luftwaffe's raid on Coventry gave a lead on which Bomber Command's bombing policy was devised.

> 'The great majority of the inhabitants of this large and important town were engaged in war industries; the light engineering industries of Coventry were almost indispensable to the production of a great range of weapons and war equipment. On the day after the raid in November 1940, production in all the war factories of the town was reduced by two-thirds. About one hundred acres in the centre of the town had been devastated. Some damage had been done to the factories themselves but it was very slight compared with the non-industrial damage. The loss of production was almost entirely due to the interruption of public utilities, the dislocation of transport, absenteeism caused by the destruction of houses, and many other causes. There was very heavy damage, for example, to sewers, water supply pipes, electric cables, gas pipes and so forth, and this had an immediate effect on production. Output was back to normal again in about two months.'*

The Germans, at the time were cock-a-hoop with their success and

---

* *Bomber Offensive*, Sir Arthur Harris.

created the word "Coventrated" as a standard for all future blitzes. Obviously they didn't realise just how their action would rebound on them many times over in the years ahead. Against the 100 acres of damage caused to Coventry, ultimately, 31 German cities had more than 500 acres of damage, and some of these – eg Berlin (6400 acres), Hamburg (6200) and many Ruhr towns and cities – received vastly more. These are revealing figures, which when compared with Coventry, indicate the amount of damage and therefore the gigantic effect it must have had on Germany's war industries. However, this is only part of the story. The relentless British/American bombing programme, day and night, forced Germany to deploy their forces to defend the Reich. For example, 20,000 anti-aircraft guns (along with millions of shells) and a supporting number of searchlight emplacements together with a multitude of radar-detection posts, all had to be maintained and manned. In addition, at one time, the greater part of the German Air Force (day and night-fighters) were engaged in defence of the Fatherland. Many hundreds of thousands of troops and personnel were engaged on these duties to the detriment of German Forces, fighting on the Russian and American/British fronts. From these facts the enormous contribution made by allied air-forces to the overall war effort is manifest.

Accordingly, at the end of the war Bomber Command and its commander-in-chief were very popular. But since then, the critics have been slowly nibbling away. Nowadays, Sir Arthur is castigated as a murderer of old people and children and is criticised for destroying the old and beautiful city of Dresden. Outside of St Clement Dane's church his statue (erected to his memory by Bomber Command's personnel) has been daubed with red paint.

The tiny minds of those who make these accusations have obviously not taken any steps to ascertain the facts. Taking the Dresden incident first, in February 1945 the Russian Army were threatening the heart of Saxony and Sir Arthur was called upon to attack the city – it was not his decision, he was directed by those above.* It was considered to be a target of primary importance. Why? Well, Dresden had by this time become the centre of communications for the defence of Germany on the southern half of the Eastern front

* *Bomber Offensive*, Sir Arthur Harris.

and it was concluded that a heavy attack would render it useless for controlling purposes. The raid did just that – it caused a fire-typhoon similar to Hamburg – and with the following two daylight raids by the Americans a vast area was laid to waste. Of course, it was a pity that such a splendid city should suffer this fate but, in war, military necessity transcends emotional judgements. However, had the raid not been carried out it seems likely that the Russians would have had to fight to take Dresden street by street and it would, thereby, have suffered the same fate. To prevent this happening and if the Germans considered it essential to preserve Dresden, why did they not declare it as an open city in advance? They could have saved it by this means ... but, perhaps their military necessities overrode all other considerations.

It is said that area bombing was responsible for the deaths of German civilians and that this was the brainchild of Sir Arthur Harris. This is quite wrong. The area bombing policy was drawn up following the raid on Coventry in late 1940 – Sir Arthur Harris was not appointed to his post as C-I-C Bomber Command until February 1942. In any case the C-I-C did not decide overall strategic policy. Decisions of this type were made by the Chiefs of Staff Committee and the War Cabinet. Contingency plans for bombing German towns were made prior to the war and the decision to manufacture four-engined bombers were at the design stage as early as 1935. None of the above can be attributed to Sir Arthur.

The bombing of German towns was a necessity – it was horrific, evil, inhuman ... it represented the worst elements found in the nature of mankind but it was essential and there was no way of preventing casualties – high casualties in many cases. The Germans used air bombing first. They had no regard for human life. They had no grounds, therefore, on which to grumble when the tables turned and they were forced to take gigantic doses of their own medicine. Sir Arthur was not to blame. He did his job as best he could and in the opinion of those who served in the Command did it very well. The blame, in fact, really lies at the feet of those who played the power game and sought to conquer the whole of Europe – Hitler and his mob.

The Second World War altered everyone's lives. It lasted for six long, wasted years – in normal times I would have spent those years consolidating my career, marrying, making a home and raising a family. Instead, in 1946, I was discharged from the RAF with a gratuity of a little more than £100 but no home, no furniture, no career and had to start from scratch to provide as best I could for my wife and two children. The government's economic problems in the post-war years (years of austerity as they were known) with the rationing of food, clothing and shortages of most essential commodities made life difficult and it was not until 1960 that generally things became easier for the family and we could settle down to a reasonably normal life – twenty-one years after the breakout of war. That's a long time to deviate from the normal path and perhaps I can be excused for saying that there is nothing for which I owe thanks to the war.

To those who criticise ex-servicemen in general, and Bomber Command's personnel in particular, let me say that I hope they live a pleasant and peaceful life which was assured by the action taken by my generation fifty or so long years ago. The glory of war? To those who think this way I sincerely hope that they don't have to find out the hard way – it's sheer hell.

Appendices

NO. 1 GROUP SUMMARY OF OPERATIONS NIGHT 20/21 APRIL, 1943
TARGET STETTIN

Detailed	70	Lancasters
Took off	70	,,
Primary	57	,,
Abortive	4	,,
Missing	8	,,
Outstanding	1	,,

PRIMARY – T.O.T. 2108 hrs – 2138 hrs.

57 Lancasters claim to have attacked the primary target dropping 57 × 4,000 lb. H.C., 2,780 × 30 lb. incend., 29,250 × 4 lb. incend., and 2,070 × 4 lb. 'X' type incend.

Weather conditions were most favourable there being no cloud, excellent visibility and bright moonlight. In these conditions crews had no difficulty in identifying the Pathfinders' Green target indicater markers which were accurately placed and most concentrated. It would appear that the earlier ones were placed in the Southern part of the town. The attack would seem to have started very punctually as by the time our first crews arrived several good fires were already established in the Southern portion of the town. These quickly gained hold and later arrivals report that the whole town was a mass of flames and that smoke from these was rising up to as high as 12,000 feet particularly from the Dock Area. Many large explosions were reported from 0118 hours onwards and the glow from the fires was seen when some of the crews were as much as 160 miles from the target on the return journey. One photograph has already been plotted just to the West of the town. Defences at the target were moderate and generally ineffective. This was not the case, however, en route where light 'Flak' was encountered not only over Denmark but also from numerous 'Flak' ships in the Baltic and the Great Belt. Reports are still incomplete but 11 aircraft were more or less severely damaged. From reports to hand at the moment fighter activity did not appear to have been considerable and no combats have been reported.

The following are extracts from Pilots' Personal Reports:-

0110 hrs.	12,000 ft.	'Green T.I.'s dead on and town getting it thick and fast.'
0111 hrs.	10,000 ft.	'Very concentrated effort – routeing very good. P.F.F. put up good show – could see Rostock burning well.'
0111 hrs.	12,000 ft.	'The most successful attack I have yet seen. It was well concentrated. P.F.F. did a good job.' 'I don't think low flying is very suitable for a target in the Baltic.'
0112 hrs.	10,000 ft.	'Very good show – P.F.F. marking excellent. Thoroughly satisfied attack successful. Large fires increasing after leaving target.'
0116 hrs.	7,000 ft.	'Very concentrated target marking and a very concentrated and successful attack.'
0120 hrs.	10,000 ft.	'Very good concentrated attack. One mass of fire. Fires still visible 160 miles distant.'

ABORTIVE:

4 Lancasters each carrying 1 × 4,000 lb. H.C. 48 × 30 lb. inc. and 540 × 4 lb. inc. abandoned mission for the following reasons:

APPENDICES

1 Lancaster owing to Starboard Inner engine being U/S jettisoned
    1 × 4,000 lb. H.C. and 48 × 30 lb. inc. safe in sea.
1 Lancaster abandoned mission at the Great Belt owing to being hit by 'Flak' and the outer port engine having caught fire. All bombs were jettisoned.
1 Lancaster damaged by heavy and light 'Flak' jettisoned its load.
1 Lancaster owing to Starboard outer engine being U/S jettisoned
    1 × 4,000 lb. H.C. and 32 × 30 lb. inc. safe in the sea.

Bibliography

MIDDLEBROOK, Martin & EVERITT, Chris: (1985) THE BOMBER COMMAND WAR DIARIES. An Operational Reference Book, 1939–1945. Viking, Penguin Books Ltd, Harmondsworth, Middlesex, England.

HARRIS, Sir Arthur: BOMBER OFFENSIVE. First published 1947 (Collins) Second edition 1990, Greenhill Books, Lional Leventhal Ltd, 1 Russell Gardens, London NW11 9NN.

PUBLIC RECORDS OFFICE: 12 Squadron Records Book. Kew, London, England.